IMAGES
of America

AROUND DANSVILLE

On the cover: The Jackson Spa is the most important institution in the history of Dansville. Once an internationally known health center, the building on the hill, although empty for the past 35 years, still looms above the town. (Town of North Dansville Historian.)

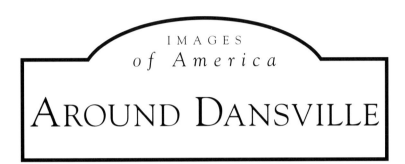

IMAGES of America
AROUND DANSVILLE

William R. Cook and Eric C. Huynh

Copyright © 2006 by William R. Cook and Eric C. Huynh
ISBN 0-7385-3708-X

Published by Arcadia Publishing
Charleston SC, Chicago IL, Portsmouth NH, San Francisco CA

Printed in the United States of America

Library of Congress Catalog Card Number: 2004111996

For all general information contact Arcadia Publishing at:
Telephone 843-853-2070
Fax 843-853-0044
E-mail sales@arcadiapublishing.com
For customer service and orders:
Toll-Free 1-888-313-2665

Visit us on the Internet at http://www.arcadiapublishing.com

Contents

Acknowledgments 6

Introduction 7

1. Main Street 9
2. Business and Industry 23
3. Civic Life 39
4. Recreation and Leisure 55
5. Home and Family 69
6. School Days 83
7. The Spa on East Hill 99
8. The Surrounding Towns of Ossian, Sparta, and West Sparta 113

ACKNOWLEDGMENTS

Books are the work of many more people than just the authors. We are grateful for the support of our friends and family. The staff at Arcadia has been enthusiastic about this project, and we thank them for that, as well as for their guidance and expertise in turning CD-ROMs and floppy disks into a book.

Most of all, we thank all of the people in and around Dansville who have allowed us to use photographs in their possession. As readers enjoy the photographs, it will be clear that our most profound thanks go to Quentin Masolotte, the historian of the town of North Dansville and hence the curator of the town's wonderful collection of photographs. Whenever we asked him if there was a picture of something we were interested in, he would always show us several. In real ways, this book is as much his as it is ours. We relied heavily on the annotations to the photograph collection made by former North Dansville town historian Wilfred Rauber. He was thorough, thoughtful, and often quite funny. We thank Livingston County historian Amie Alden for her help and advice. We are grateful to Rhea Walker, Mary Jo Marks, and David Palmer, town historians in, respectively, Ossian, Sparta, and West Sparta. Special thanks go to those individuals who granted us access to their personal treasures and permission to use them.

From the beginning, we had the support of North Dansville's town supervisor, Dennis Mahus, and we appreciate his interest in seeing the work come to fruition.

It is to the people of Dansville that we owe the most thanks. They have welcomed us and supported us as we did our research and brought the book to completion. This book, in the most profound way, is theirs.

INTRODUCTION

There is not a great deal of information available about Capt. Dan Faulkner. However, we know a lot about the town that bears his name: Dansville. For more than 200 years, Dansville has been a regional center for southern Livingston and northern Steuben Counties. Dansville has also been a town whose people and goods and influence have reached far beyond this region.

More than once, Dansville has reinvented itself; it has been an agricultural center, an industrial center, and a service center, although there is a great deal of overlap. The Jackson Spa gave way to Foster-Wheeler, which in turn gave way to Noyes Memorial Hospital as the town's chief employer and claim to fame. Still, Dansville is a town rooted in and respectful of its storied past.

If we focus on change, consider some of the professions practiced in Dansville in 1868: boatman, hoopskirt manufacturer, Canaseraga stagecoach operator, grape grower, dealer in sheepskins, manufacturer of imitation whalebone, and superintendent of the trout pond. But this is only half the story. There were many medical professionals, shopkeepers, teachers, and even photographers, just as there are today.

When Dansville's residents have put their minds to improving their town, they have succeeded. The most famous example of this is the victorious struggle to have the Dansville cut of the Genesee Valley Canal come right to Main Street. The fact that 160 years later there is still a Battle Street in downtown Dansville is testimony to how far the town's citizens were willing to go to get what they needed to prosper. In more recent times, whether the issue is the beautification of Main Street, the upgrading of the airport, the expansion of the hospital, the establishment of festivals, or the renewal of industrial production, Dansville forges ahead until the mission is accomplished.

Most of the chapters in *Around Dansville* have themes that are those of every town—Main Street, businesses, school, and so forth. Of course, Dansville's Main Street, businesses, and schools are unique, but there are close parallels with other towns throughout western New York and beyond. However, we chose to devote a chapter to the spa on East Hill, which was known by several different names. It is the signature institution of Dansville. It brought Dansville international notoriety and was directly responsible for the arrival of Dansville's most famous citizen, Clara Barton, in 1876. Even though the spa has been closed for 35 years, it literally and figuratively looms over Dansville.

When we undertook this project, we did so both with confidence and a certain trepidation. William has previously written two books of local history, including *Around Geneseo* with Arcadia Publishing and *Celebrating Our Past: Livingston County in the Twentieth Century*. Eric has high-level computer skills and is currently a senior majoring in history at Wabash College. In addition, we knew of the splendid photograph collection maintained by North Dansville's town historian Quentin Masolotte, and he has been strongly supportive of our effort to publish many photographs from that collection.

Our concern was that we are not Dansvillians. Sometimes folks are a bit uneasy about "outsiders" writing their history. However, we are from just up the road in Geneseo, the county seat of Livingston County. Our family has had many experiences in Dansville. William first visited it just a few days after he moved to Geneseo in 1970. Eric has played varsity sports against the Dansville Mustangs. We have visited members of our family at Noyes Memorial Hospital. More important, the people with whom we have worked on this project have been supportive. Ever since we were given the opportunity to create this book, Dansvillians have been eager to see it published. Although a few of the photographs appear in *Celebrating Our Past* and several others have been featured in the *Genesee Country Express* over a period of 30 years, this is the first time they have been gathered together in one place and printed with the finest technology and on sturdy paper. And there are many never-before-published pictures. This book will teach history and bring back memories to the people of Dansville and to many whose families have roots there.

There are too many wonderful old photographs of Dansville to fit into this book. Despite this, we believe that it is important to place Dansville in its proper rural context. Hence, we decided that the book was incomplete without having a look at the three Livingston County towns that border Dansville—Ossian, Sparta, and West Sparta. The historians of those three towns generously supplied photographs for *Celebrating Our Past,* and we are grateful that they have continued to make them available. We know that a good case can be made for including the towns of Wayland, Cohocton, and Dansville in Steuben County, but we chose to confine this book to Livingston County. Note: Those who are not intimately familiar with Dansville will find it useful to know that the village of Dansville is located in the town of North Dansville, Livingston County.

We hope that the publication of this book will stimulate new interest in Dansville's storied past. Perhaps schoolteachers can use it in their classrooms and take students on adventures to find what some of those buildings pictured in it look like now. Hopefully older family members will share memories with younger ones who look at the book and add their personal captions to those accompanying the photographs on each page. If this book contributes even a bit to stimulate pride and interest in Dansville and to encourage preservation of the town's heritage, then we are well rewarded for our time. We offer this book to the people of Dansville with respect for what has been and high expectation for what is to come.

—William R. Cook and Eric C. Huynh

One
Main Street

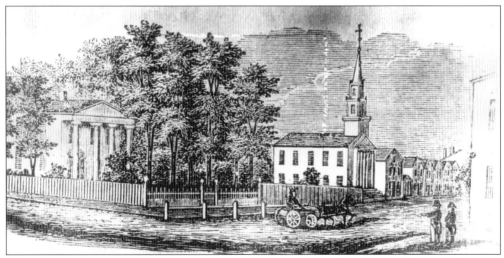

This drawing was made between 1831 and 1841 and shows the corner of Main and Perine Streets. People familiar with Dansville now will recognize the building on the left, the Memorial Library. At the time of the drawing, it was the Shepard home, given to the village for a library almost a century later. The church is the first Presbyterian church in Dansville. It, together with the buildings behind it, was destroyed by a fire in 1851. There is a certain quaintness to this early image of Dansville. (Town of North Dansville Historian.)

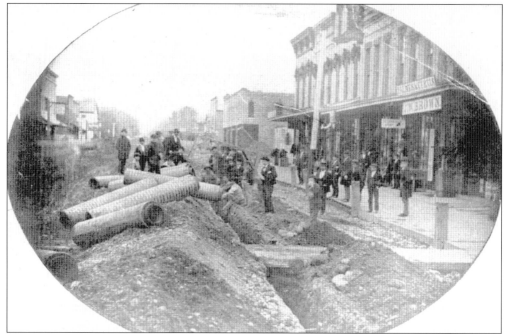

Four decades later, Main Street required infrastructure in order for it to remain a center of commerce. This photograph, also from Main and Perine Streets, is from the 1870s and shows the installation of a water main under Main Street. (Town of North Dansville Historian.)

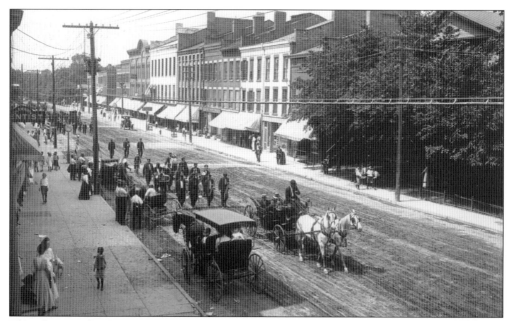

This photograph of Main Street in the first decade of the 20th century shows a parade that few people are paying attention to. The street is still not paved, although there are crosswalks. It may be that this was sufficient for the horse-drawn carts, but the early automobile is a visible reminder of imminent change. Note that there are prominent telephone lines. (Town of North Dansville Historian.)

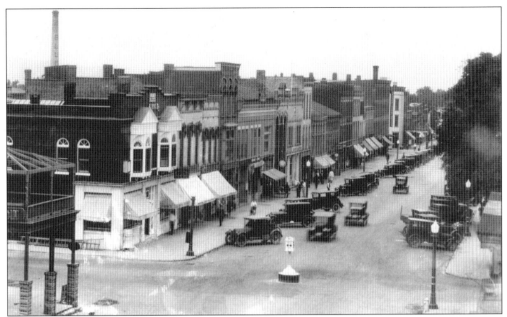

Main Street has changed by the time this photograph was taken about 20 years later. It is paved, and there are many automobiles. There is even a traffic signal in the middle of the intersection of Main and Clara Barton Streets. The building on the left bears the sign "Kramer Block 1890" at the top. The smokestack to the west of Main Street in the background is that of the Blum Shoe factory. (Town of North Dansville Historian.)

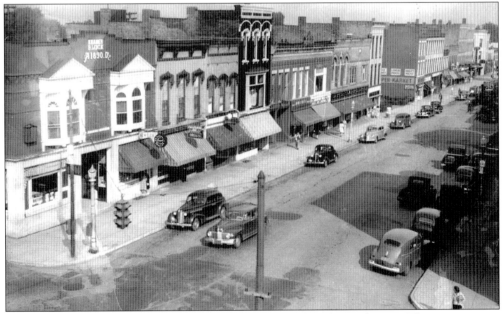

A generation after the previous photograph, Main Street has changed again. The cars are more modern, of course, and there is a stoplight hanging over the intersection of Main and Clara Barton Streets. A parking lot provides space for those driving to the supermarket on Main Street. Today grocery shopping is primarily done in large stores away from Main Street. (Town of North Dansville Historian.)

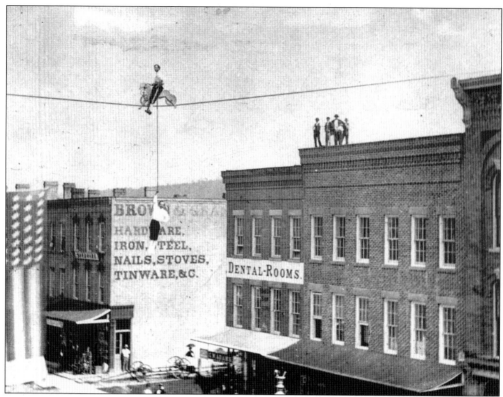

In 1875, the Allen brothers performed high above the crowd without a net. The man hanging is providing balance for his brother on the bicycle. Notice Brown's hardware and the much feared Dental Rooms in the background. (Town of North Dansville Historian.)

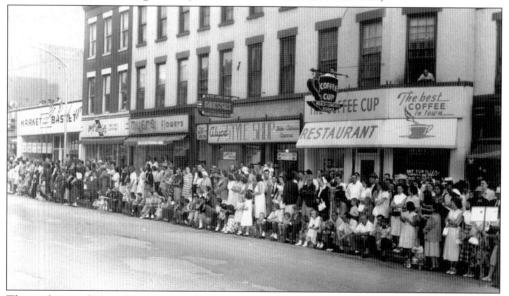

The tradition of Main Street as a gathering place for special events has continued in Dansville. Here a large crowd of all ages waits for a parade. There are even people watching from windows and from the roof of the Market Basket. (Town of North Dansville Historian.)

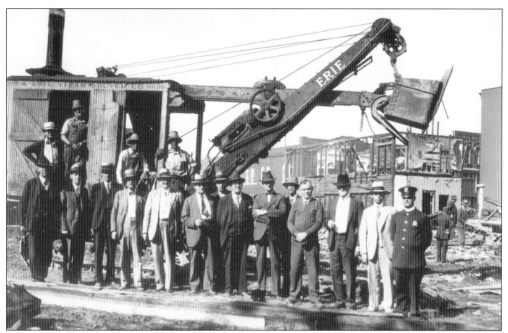

Although some of the buildings seen in the previous pictures survive and give an elegance and sense of tradition to those who visit Main Street, change is necessary. In 1932, the new post office is being constructed at the corner of Main and Clara Barton Streets. (Town of North Dansville Historian.)

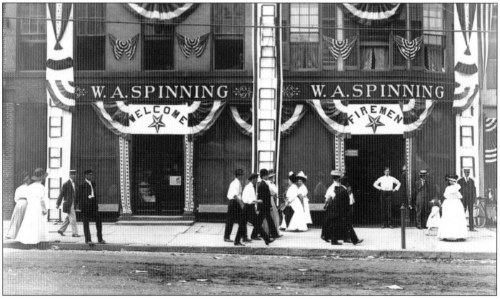

There were many meetings and conventions held in Dansville. For example, in 1902, German-speaking Catholics from throughout New York gathered in Dansville, a town with a strong German heritage. Seven years later, the firemen of western New York held a convention in Dansville, and local merchants decorated their Main Street stores. W. A. Spinning's store sold dry goods. It stood where, for many years, the Coffee Cup restaurant was later located. (Town of North Dansville Historian.)

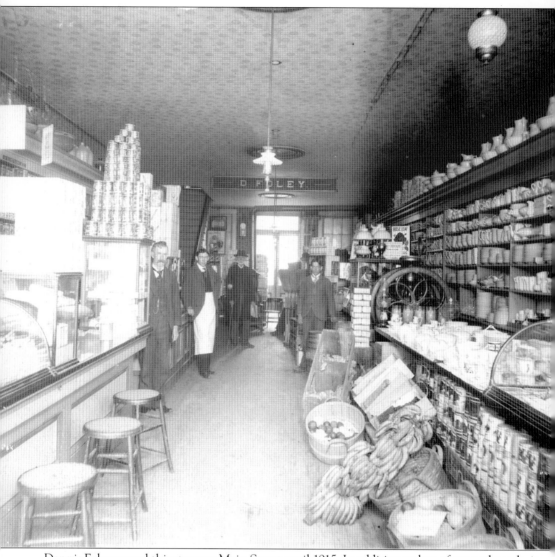

Dennis Foley owned this store on Main Street until 1915. In addition to lots of canned goods, it sold fresh fruit, including bananas. They no doubt arrived in Dansville by rail. From the shelves on the right, one could conclude that people in Dansville broke lots of crockery. In the back behind the old gentleman is a potbellied stove and several chairs. No doubt issues from next door to across the globe were discussed around that stove. (Town of North Dansville Historian.)

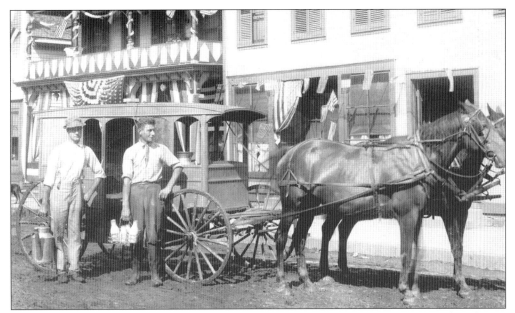

Milk was delivered both in bottles and in a can. Perhaps this photograph was taken during a celebration, but it appears from many such photographs that patriotic decorations were continuously a part of Dansville's life. (Town of North Dansville Historian.)

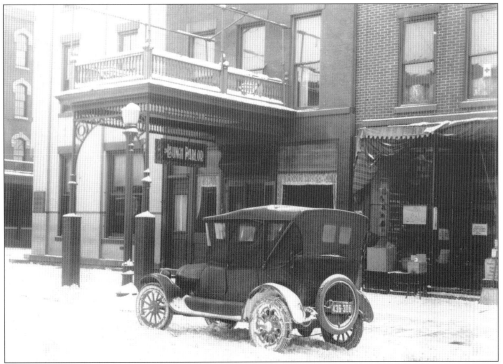

The Lunch Parlor had this lovely portico until 1925, when a car lost control and smashed into it. Other porticos on Main Street suffered the same fate. The Rauber and Robards grocery store is on the right. The car has chains on the left rear tire, and side curtains have been installed for the winter. (Town of North Dansville Historian.)

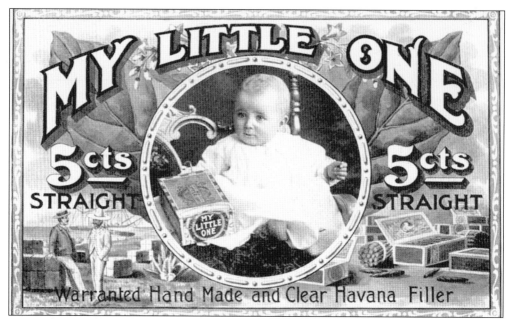

This advertisement for Dansville-manufactured cigars from 1902 is a reminder of how sensibilities change. Imagine an advertisement for cigars featuring a baby with a cigar box in hand! On the left, the advertisement imagines a tranquil Havana harbor only four years after the USS *Maine* was blown up there, leading to the Spanish-American War. (Rochester Roman Catholic Diocese.)

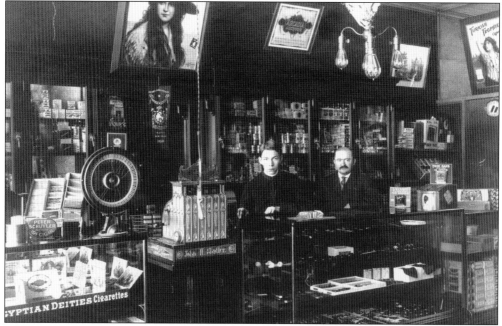

Charles Rausch and probably his son stand in his newly purchased cigar store. The banner under the large picture in the center wishes everyone Merry Christmas and Happy New Year in 1910. There are all sorts of tobacco products with such exotic brand names as Turkish Trophies and Egyptian Deities. The cash register bears the name of John Stadtler, the previous owner. (Town of North Dansville Historian.)

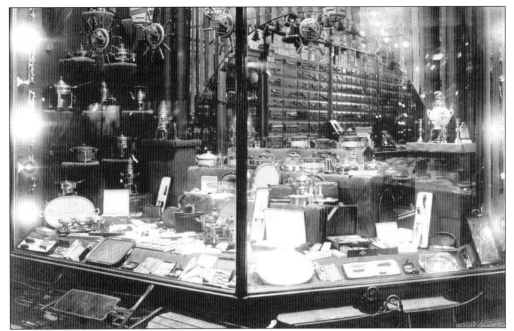

George Peck's store window is decorated for Christmas in 1915. Although most of the gift items displayed are such things as chafing dishes and casseroles, there are some whittling knives in the window and sleds outside underneath it. The numerous drawers visible through the window are for various hardware items. (Town of North Dansville Historian.)

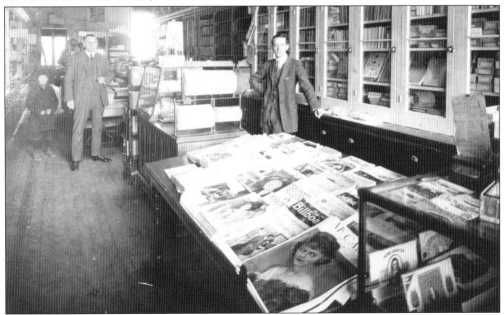

Herman DeLong Jr. is shown as the proprietor of the family's bookstore in 1918. In addition to books, the store sold magazines. In view are *Billboard* and *McCall's*, both quite elegant publications. Next to them is a magazine about poultry. In the right foreground are the ubiquitous boxes of cigars. This store was located in the Maxwell Block on the east side of Main Street; there is still a bookstore in the Maxwell Block in 2006. (Town of North Dansville Historian.)

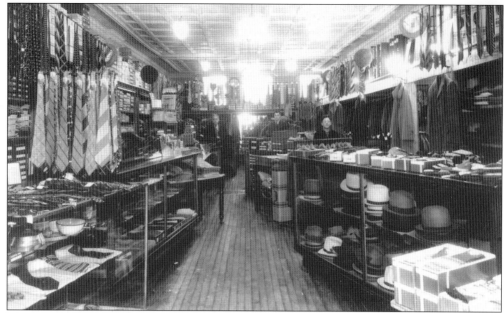

The Rauber and Maloney store on Main Street specialized in clothes for men. Obviously hats and neckties were popular items. The latter decorate the entire upper gallery of the store. Somewhat incongruously, in the case above the white shirts with ties on the left, is a collection of camping goods, including a mess kit and a first aid kit. This photograph was taken in 1938. (Town of North Dansville Historian.)

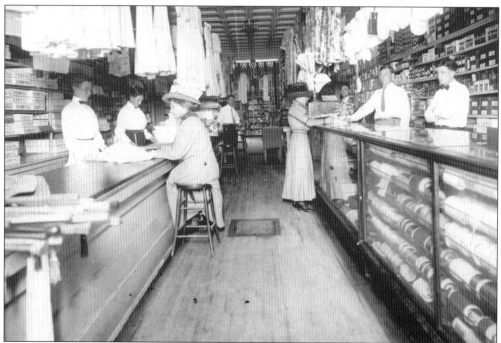

Other stores were exclusively for women. In this establishment are both ready-made clothes and the materials for making clothes at home; especially prominent are the ribbons and buttons being sold at the right counter. (Town of North Dansville Historian.)

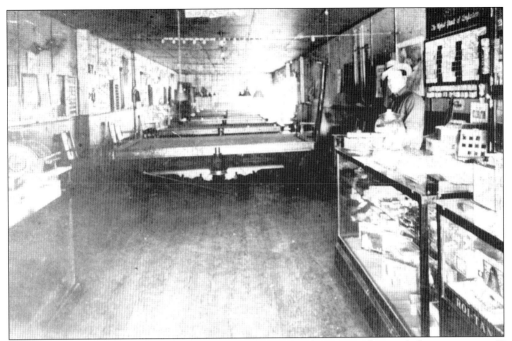

What town would be complete without a place for the "boys" to relax and shoot some pool? Since the case on the right contains cigars, it is easy to imagine a blue haze hanging there in the evenings. (Town of North Dansville Historian.)

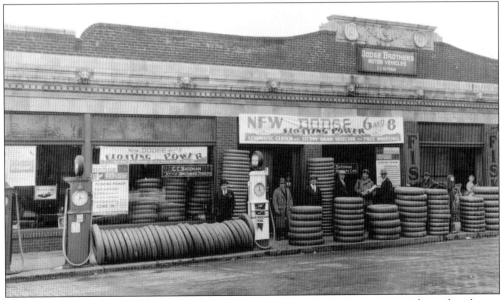

The automobile changed the way of shopping and thus Main Street, as evidenced today in Dansville's outskirts where one finds large stores and restaurants. C. C. Bateman sold Dodge automobiles and trucks. One of the signs in the window advertises the 1932 models. The large banner promotes the "automatic clutch and silent gear selector" (automatic transmission) vehicles for sale. Bateman apparently sold a lot of tires and also had two gas pumps. (Town of North Dansville Historian.)

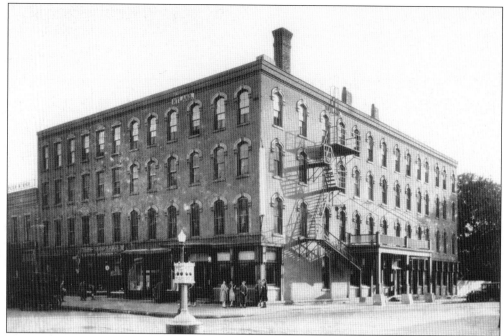

One of the grand Main Street buildings was the Hyland House Hotel, located at the corner of Main and Clara Barton Streets. Later it was called the Foster Club Hotel and still later the Hotel Dansville (with a large Dansville neon sign). The early stoplight in the intersection is the same one in the photograph on page 11. (Town of North Dansville Historian.)

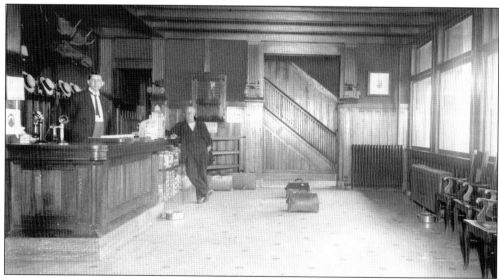

This 1911 photograph shows the lobby of the Hyland House. It is well equipped with chairs, a counter that sells—what else—cigars, and two spittoons. Behind the desk is a series of stylish straw hats and above them an enormous moose head. All in all, it is quite a manly place. It is interesting that there are two telephones on the counter because Dansville had two separate telephone systems at the time, and the hotel was connected to both. (Town of North Dansville Historian.)

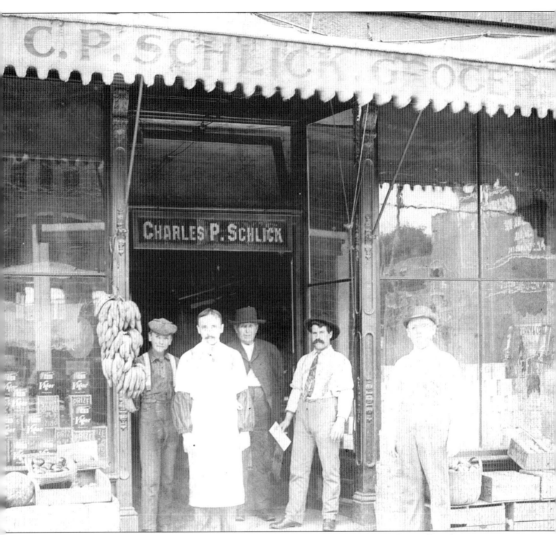

Charles Schlick's grocery store was located in the same building as the Hyland House. In this 1902 photograph is a variety of locally grown produce—eggplants and potatoes and watermelons—juxtaposed with the exotic bunch of rather ripe bananas. The boxes in the left window appear to contain dry cereal. Since one major form of dry cereal was invented in Dansville at Dr. James C. Jackson's sanatorium, it is not surprising that the people of Dansville would be attracted to this display of several varieties of breakfast cereal. (Town of North Dansville Historian.)

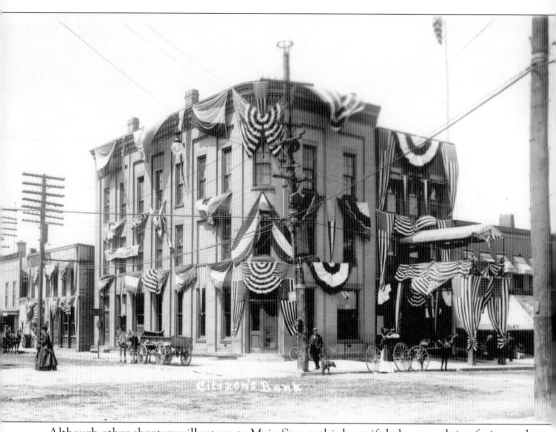

Although other chapters will return to Main Street, this beautiful photograph is a fitting end to the chapter devoted to the heart of Dansville. Here the town is decked out patriotically. This was the Citizen's Bank on the corner of Main and Ossian Streets; later the bank moved across the street and a bit farther north, but the original building still stands proudly. It is interesting to see that although the car has not yet replaced the horse and the street is of course unpaved, the new technology is quite evident in the power and telephone lines and the fire hydrant at the far right. (Town of North Dansville Historian.)

Two
BUSINESS AND INDUSTRY

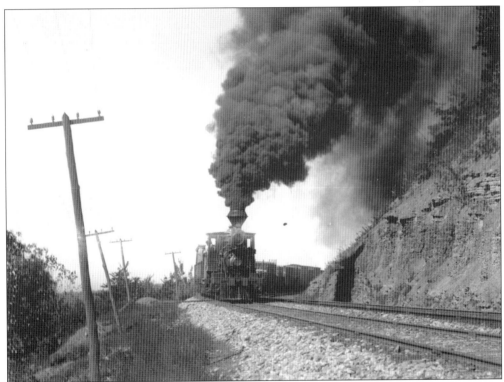

The previous chapter showed some of the practical results of better transportation, especially the railroad. The fact that people in Dansville could buy bananas from the Caribbean is one obvious example. However, the railroad was even more important for the development of manufacturing in Dansville. In this photograph, the steam engine of the Lackawanna Railroad comes toward Dansville. The first railroad arrived in the 1870s. (Town of North Dansville Historian.)

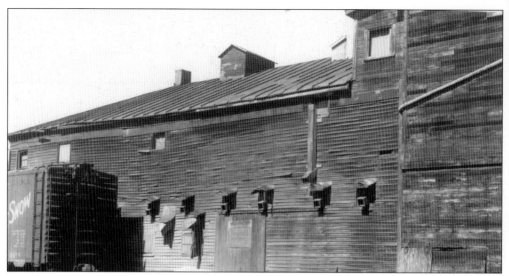

There was an earlier revolution in transportation, however, that led to the prosperity of Livingston County and the Genesee Valley. The Genesee Valley Canal was built to connect this fertile area to the Erie Canal in Rochester. At Sonyea, the canal turned southwest toward Nunda and what became Letchworth State Park. There was a cut made to connect Dansville to the canal. However, the merchants of the town were dissatisfied with the fact it did not come all the way to Main Street. Dansvillians dug their own "extension" of the canal. When the state refused to authorize it, men of Dansville dug through to connect it to the canal. The so-called Battle of Dansville was won. This photograph shows a warehouse that was alongside the canal before it was filled in. The spouts along the building allowed grain to go from the warehouse directly into canal boats. The train car sits where the canal was. (Town of North Dansville Historian.)

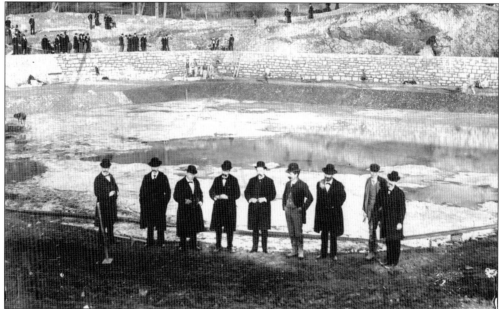

Another important factor in the development of industry in Dansville was plentiful and reliable water. In 1897, Dansville's first reservoir was dedicated. It was fed by a natural spring that was owned by Dr. James C. Jackson and the sanatorium. (Town of North Dansville Historian.)

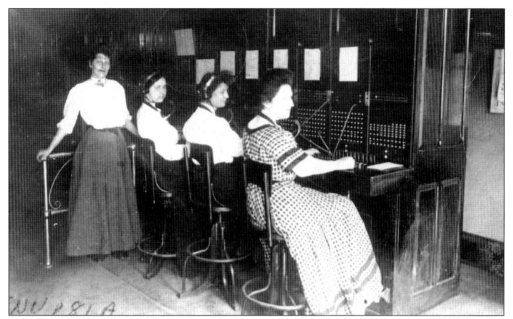

In addition to transportation and water, businesses profited from greatly improved communications. Previous pages have shown the telephone wires on Main Street and the telephones in the Hyland House Hotel. These New York Bell operators served Dansville when this photograph was taken in 1908. (Town of North Dansville Historian.)

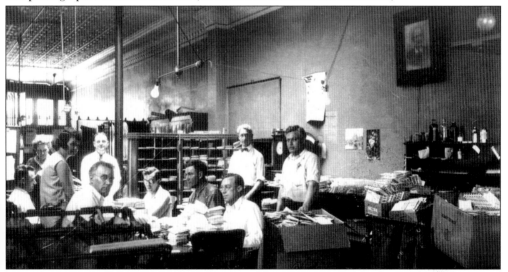

Another key part of the change in communications was in the improvement of postal service throughout the United States. However, the Dansville Post Office appears to be swamped in this 1931 photograph. This was due to the celebration of the 50th anniversary of the founding of the American Red Cross in Dansville. A commemorative stamp was issued, and thousands of interested people and stamp collectors wrote for first day of issue cancellations. Edward Murphy (right) worked for the post office for more than a half century before retiring in 1951. He beat the longevity record of Henry Sedgwick, who died in 1892 after working in the post office for 46 years. Sedgwick's portrait hangs on the wall on the right in this photograph. A year later, a new post office was under construction (see page 13). (Town of North Dansville Historian.)

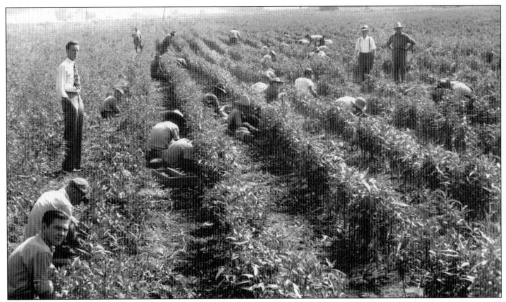

The nursery business began in Dansville in the 1850s. As early as 1880, Dr. James C. Jackson at the sanatorium began to develop nurseries that would produce fresh flowers and vegetables for his clients. A generation later, the nursery business was one of the most important in Dansville, employing hundreds and shipping products throughout the United States and Canada. Many of the employees were boys and young men who got their first taste of work in the nurseries. These employees are working with small cherry trees. It was an important skill to implant a bud of a particular variety onto the young tree. (Town of North Dansville Historian.)

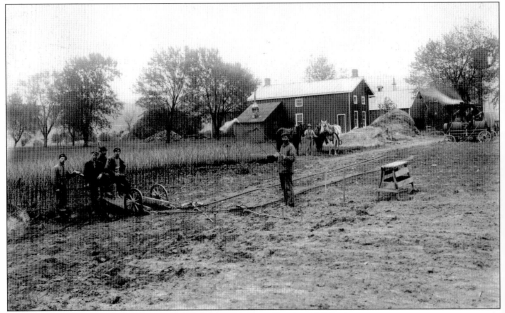

The nursery business made use of new technologies. In this field where trees were grown, a steam engine is being used to dig trenches for the planting of more trees. The steam engine pulled cables attached to a plow. The engine is fired up, and the man in the middle is giving flag signals to start the winding of the cables. (Town of North Dansville Historian.)

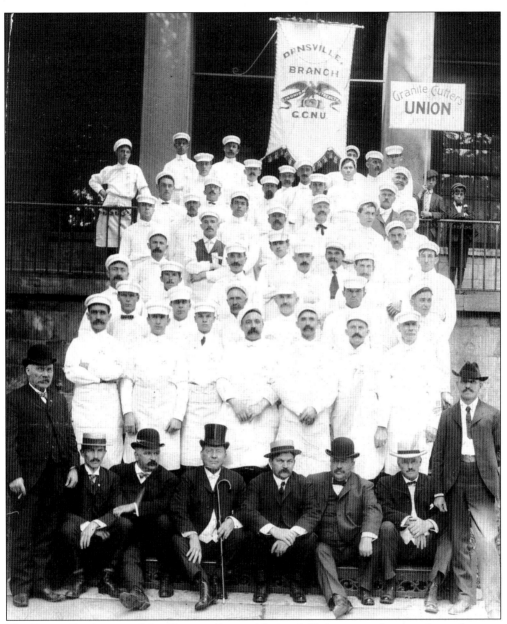

The Dansville chapter of the Granite Cutters National Union was a large and proud group, as seen in this undated photograph. The national union was formed in 1877, and its heyday in western New York was over by about 1910. A poem from the union's national magazine tells why a woman would prefer a stonecutter to a merchant, farmer, carpenter, blacksmith, or sailor: "But, just give me a stonecutter— / a fellow true and fine; / Who neither drinks, or smokes, or swears. / Ah! that's the man for me; / I know we'd lead a lovely life; / Yes, I would be a stonecutter's wife." One might wonder whether these men were really quite that virtuous doing their hard and dangerous work. (Town of North Dansville Historian.)

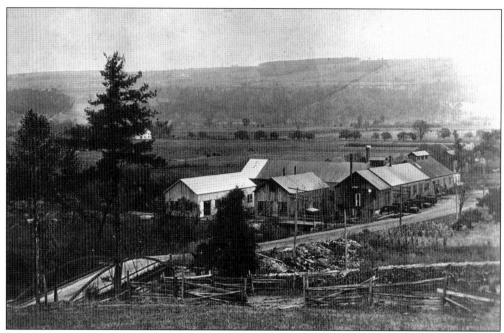

As early as the 1830s, Warren Cummins established a foundry in the area that has come to be known as Cumminsville. Around 1900, Pell Foster Sr. established the Power Specialty Company. Here is an early picture of the budding industrial complex. Much of the power was generated from the creek flowing in front of the buildings. (Town of North Dansville Historian.)

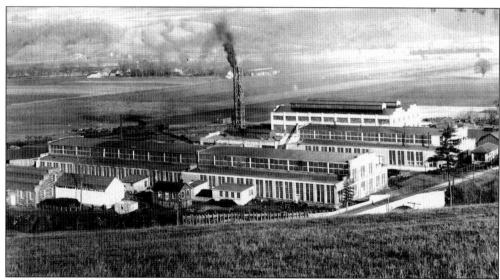

In 1927, Power Speciality merged with Wheeler Condenser and Engineering Company to create Foster-Wheeler. Although Foster-Wheeler closed at the beginning of the 21st century, the facility currently is in the process of becoming a productive place once again. Note the white house in the left distance, showing that this and the previous photograph were taken from precisely the same spot. (Town of North Dansville Historian.)

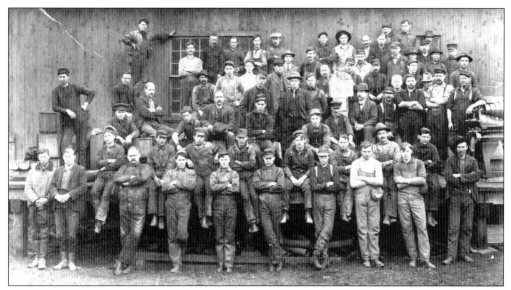

Power Specialty employed many. Here employees pose, probably to celebrate either the initiation or completion of a major contract. (Town of North Dansville Historian.)

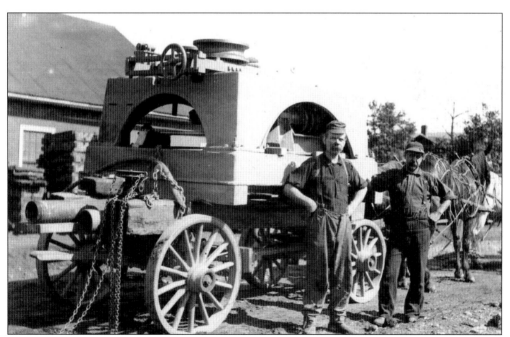

Power Specialty used and made large metal objects such as boilers. The stuff was heavy. The image tends to elicit a certain sympathy for the horses that are so carefully rigged to pull this cart. (Town of North Dansville Historian.)

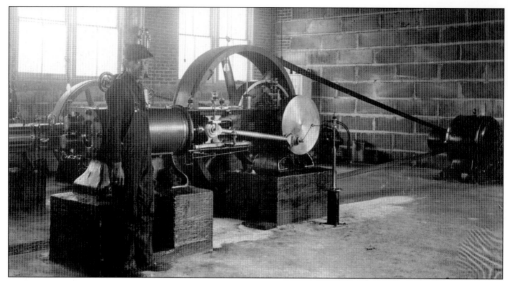

In 1914, the George Sweet Manufacturing Company was bought by Power Specialty. In 1911, it had opened a new building with new power technology designed to replace water as the source of power. This photograph shows some of the new technology and the man who operated it, Joe Gerber. (Town of North Dansville Historian.)

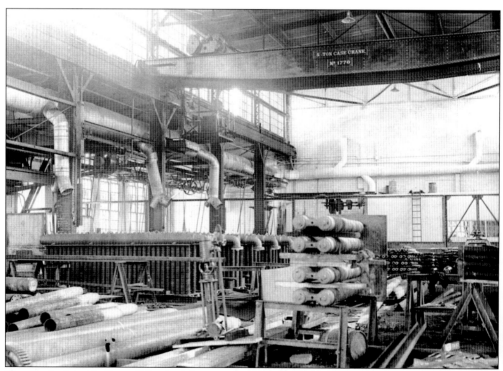

Here is a look inside Foster-Wheeler. The complexity and vastness of the operation is impressive. The crane across the top of the photograph could move five tons. (Town of North Dansville Historian.)

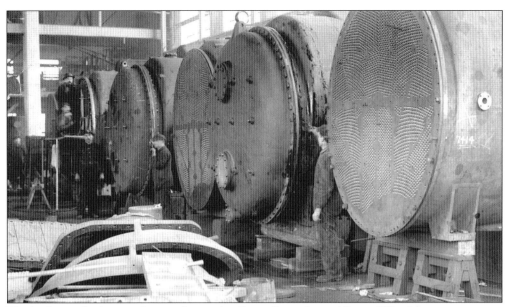

The boilers and other goods manufactured at Power Specialty and Foster-Wheeler were important at any time, but especially at times when the nation was at war. Pell Foster Sr. used this photograph while giving speeches to illustrate how his factory helped to win World War I. The factory operated around the clock and produced equipment for the navy that made it safer for American ships to get supplies to the troops "over there." (Town of North Dansville Historian.)

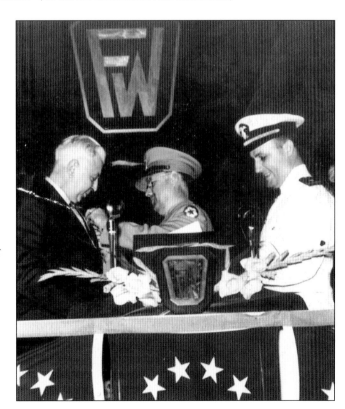

In August 1942, Foster-Wheeler (note logo in background) received the prestigious E (for excellence) award from the United States government for its production of war supplies. Frank Schledorn, a member of the workforce, represents his colleagues in receiving a lapel pin with the letter E. (Town of North Dansville Historian.)

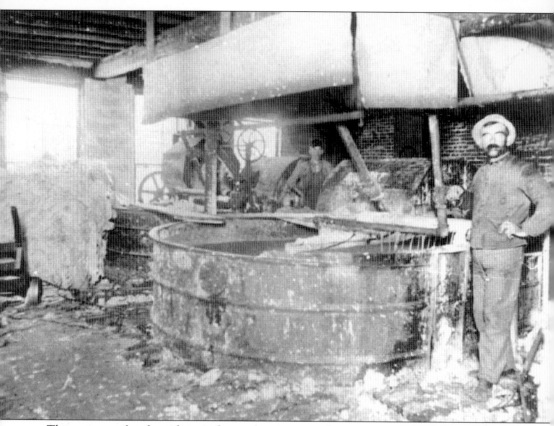

This may not be the tidiest industry, but it certainly was an important one. Papermaking complemented the publishing business, which flourished in Dansville. The factory, long ago destroyed, can be seen behind a golfer in a photograph on page 62. (Town of North Dansville Historian.)

The Owen Publishing Company played an important role in Dansville's economy. It was a premier publisher of educational materials both for schools and individuals. Here is the composing room in 1904. (Town of North Dansville Historian.)

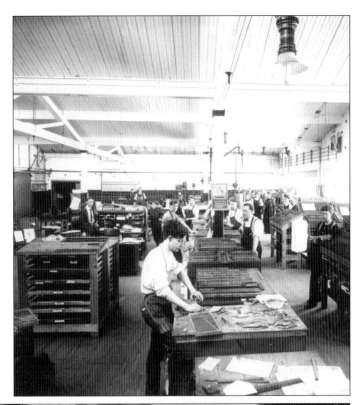

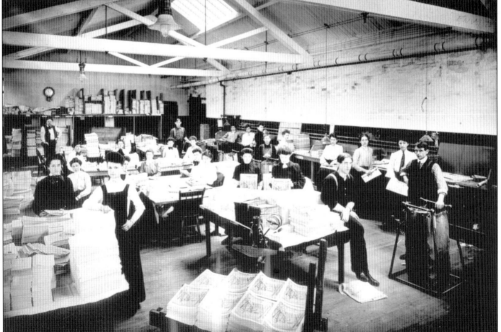

The scale of Owen's capacity is clear from this photograph of the production area. The railroad was vital for the development of this as well as so many other businesses in Dansville. (Town of North Dansville Historian.)

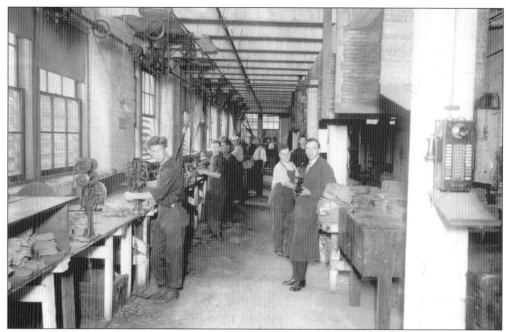

Footwear made at the Blum Shoe Manufacturing Company was shipped throughout the United States, as illustrated in a photograph on page 67 of a float that Blum created for a parade in Dansville. The photograph here shows shoemakers at work. In 1911, Blum produced 350,000 pairs of shoes. (Town of North Dansville Historian.)

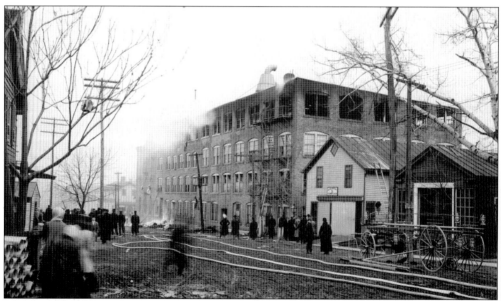

Shoe production in Dansville literally went up in smoke. Piles of smoldering felt are on the ground in front of the left end of the building, and some pieces are hanging above the piles on wires. The fire truck is on the right and oddly sports a bowler hat just to the left of the ladder leaning against the veterinarian's office. Probably a member of the Fearless Hose came directly from his job and traded that formal chapeau for a fireman's helmet. (Town of North Dansville Historian.)

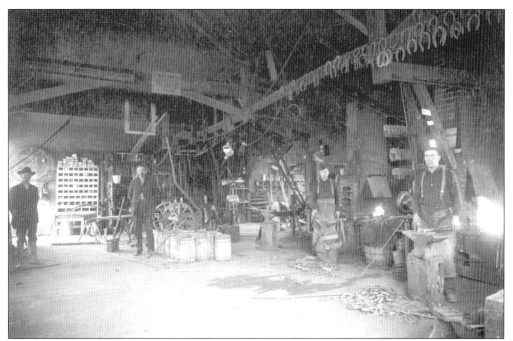

Although not every town had a publisher or shoe factory or large power equipment manufacturing, all had blacksmith shops. Here is one in Dansville. (Town of North Dansville Historian.)

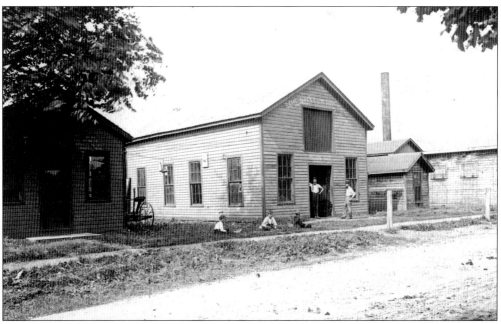

This photograph shows the Samuel Allen and Son Manufacturing Company's machine shop. The company specialized in making tags. It moved from Dansville but not too far. The Allen-Bailey Tag Company still operates in Caledonia. (Town of North Dansville Historian.)

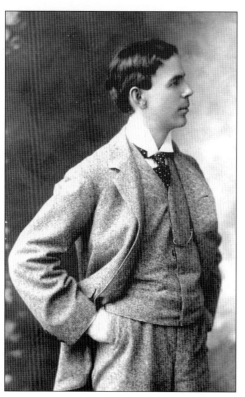

This handsome young fellow is John Klink, seen in a photograph from 1898. Klink became interested in the automobile and created one that was manufactured in Dansville. In retrospect, perhaps Klink is not a good name for a car. Even though only a few were made, the Klink is listed among the 5,342 types of automobile that have been manufactured around the world. (Town of North Dansville Historian.)

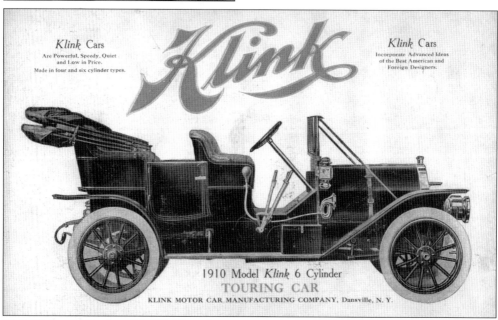

This Klink sold for about $2,000. The advertisement claimed that it used the latest in American and foreign ingenuity. John Klink brought a native of western New York, Charles H. Day, from California to be superintendent and designing engineer. Day later became an important figure in the development of aviation, among other things designing the first laminated wood propellers. (Town of North Dansville Historian.)

This is a beautiful photograph of Robert Dotterweich, the proprietor of the Dansville Brewery Company. Given Dansville's German heritage, it is natural that a brewery would be established here. Beer was brewed in Dansville before Dansville Brewing Company was founded in 1888, but it was between 1890 and 1910 that manufacturing reached its height. (Town of North Dansville Historian.)

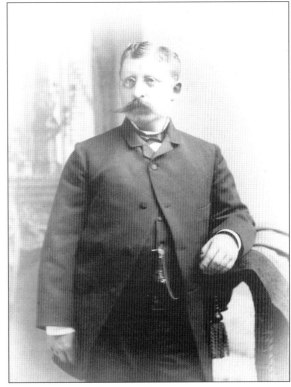

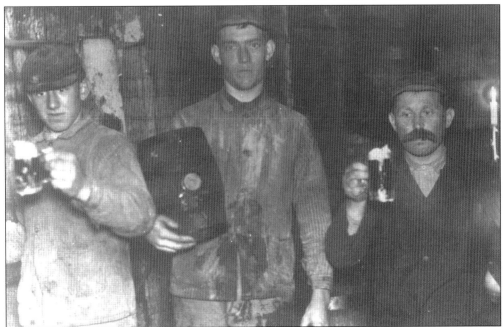

This photograph was taken during the brewery's heyday in the 1890s. Brewmaster Sebastian Sommer (right) and two employees are enjoying their premier product, Mountain Dew lager beer. People in Dansville were saying "Give me a Dew" a century before the popular commercial for a soft drink of the same name. (Town of North Dansville Historian.)

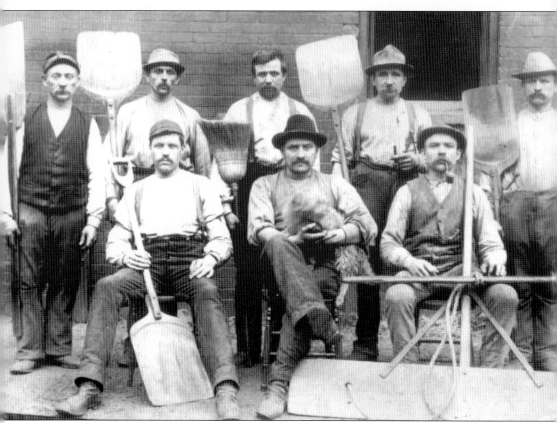

Brewmaster Sebastian Sommer sits with a dog on his lap—a dog that did not sit still enough while the photograph was being taken—surrounded by workers holding various tools of the brewery trade. (Town of North Dansville Historian.)

Three
CIVIC LIFE

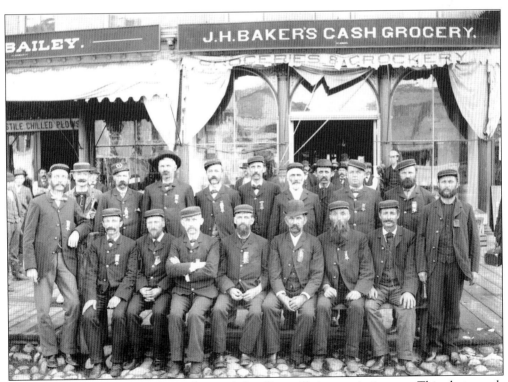

It is clear from the photographs in chapter 1 that Dansville is a patriotic town. This photograph of a group of Civil War veterans was taken on Main Street (note the cobblestones and wooden sidewalk). Some men wear their army caps, and all wear badges. Since there is only one graybeard in the group, it seems likely that this photograph was taken about the time of the chartering of the Seth Hedges Post of the Grand Army of the Republic (GAR) in 1881, the first such post in Livingston County. (Town of North Dansville Historian.)

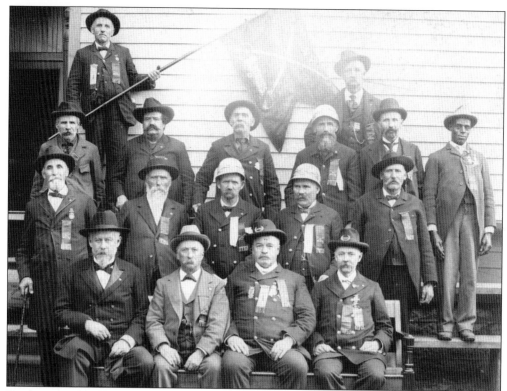

By the time this photograph was taken, Dansville's Civil War veterans had grown older. The banner is of the New York Dragoons. It is interesting that there is an African American veteran at the right. He did not fight in the same unit as the white men, but they all fought for the same cause. (Town of North Dansville Historian.)

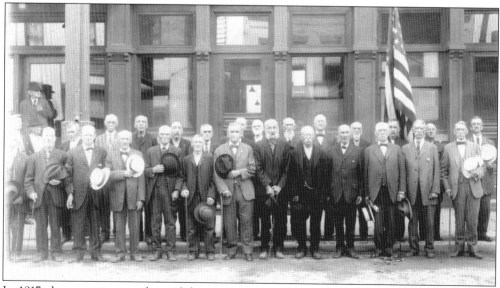

In 1917, the surviving members of the GAR gathered once again on Main Street as America entered another war, World War I. When this picture was taken, the Civil War had been over for 52 years. (Town of North Dansville Historian.)

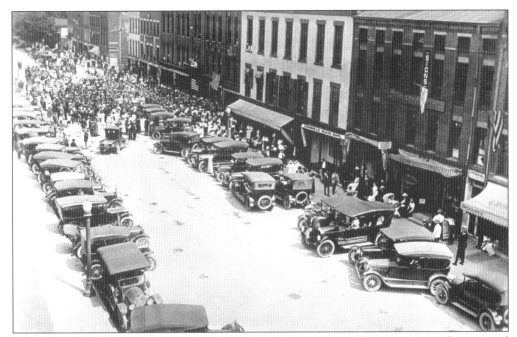

On July 16, 1917, Dansvillians gathered on Main Street to provide a rousing and emotional send-off to young men who were going off to war. Following official ceremonies, the enlistees were driven to the Lackawanna station for a final farewell. (Town of North Dansville Historian.)

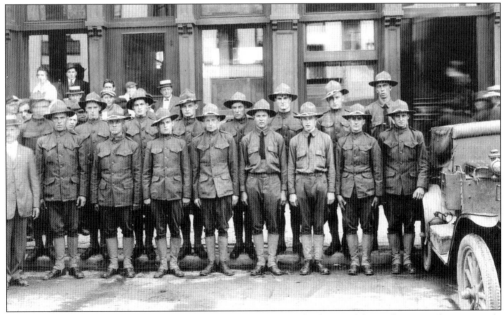

These brave doughboys pose where the GAR members had posed (see photograph opposite). There was a war between the Civil War and World War I, and Dansville played its part in that conflict too. Not only did Dansvillians serve, but the Red Cross chapter provided needed bandages and mosquito netting to the men in the Philippines and the Caribbean. (Town of North Dansville Historian.)

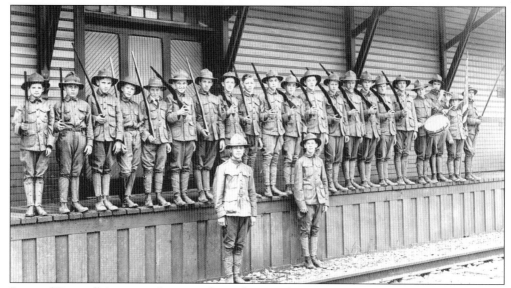

Some of Dansville's teenage boys are shown here at the train station as members of the Cadet Corps, complete with fife and drum at the right. This corps was probably modeled on Robert Baden-Powell's establishment of a defense corps of Boy Scouts in England when the Great War began in 1914. (Town of North Dansville Historian.)

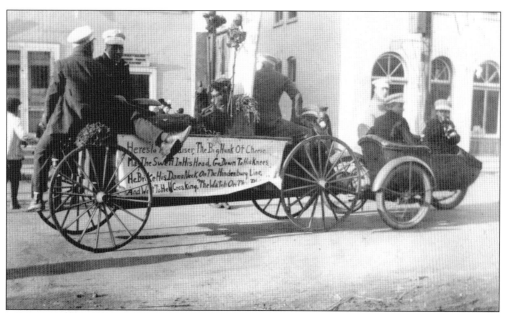

All over America, citizens turned out to watch hastily arranged parades when news of the end of World War I (November 11, 1918) was announced. In this float, Dansville, a city with many German Americans, showed that it was as American as apple pie. The text reads, "Here's to the kaiser, the big hunk of cheese, may the swell in his head go down to his knees. He broke his damn neck on the Hinderburg Line and went to hell croaking 'The Watch on the Rhine.'" This last line refers to a patriotic German song about always defending the Rhine River. (Town of North Dansville Historian.)

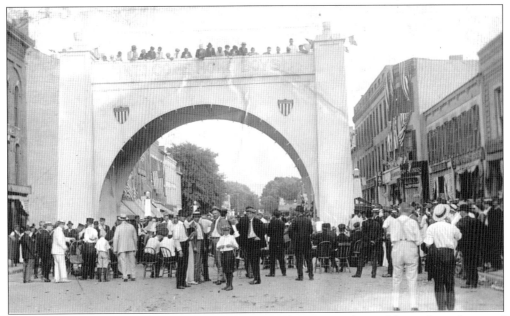

When Dansville's boys returned from "over there," they were welcomed home by a throng of people and a triumphal arch constructed on Main Street bearing the simple words "Welcome Home Boys." (Town of North Dansville Historian.)

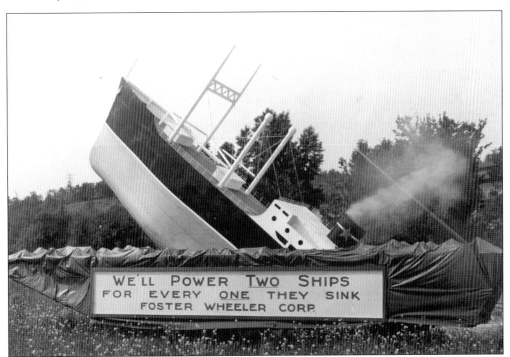

Before the World War I veterans turned gray, America was at war again, fighting in Europe, Africa, and Asia. Foster-Wheeler provided some of the equipment that led to victory on all fronts in 1945. Shown here is a large decoration that Foster-Wheeler made to demonstrate its importance and its resolve during World War II. (Town of North Dansville Historian.)

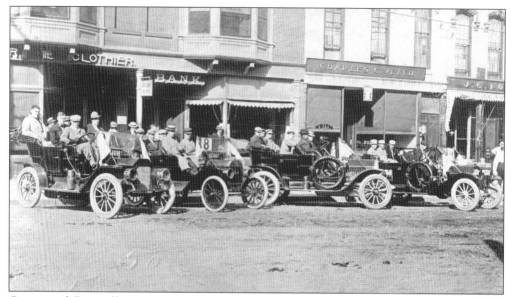

Citizens of Dansville participated in a wide range of civic activities. With Main Street as the gathering point, folks bring their vehicles to a car rally about 1910. (Town of North Dansville Historian.)

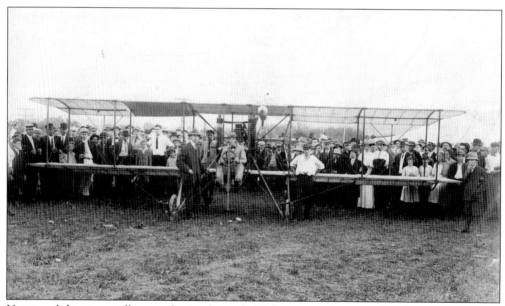

If automobiles were still a novelty in the early 20th century, imagine the excitement in 1911 when this airplane landed in Dansville, the first in Livingston County. From that time until the present, Dansville has been the aviation center of the area. One person present in 1911 and probably in this photograph was Lynn Pickard. Later he founded the Dansville Airport (official abbreviation DSV). It was used to train military personnel during World War II. The first air freight sent from the airport was a piece of equipment made at Foster-Wheeler to Indianapolis in 1948. Charles Lindbergh once landed in Dansville. In recent times, the airport has been used primarily for private planes and gliders. (Town of North Dansville Historian.)

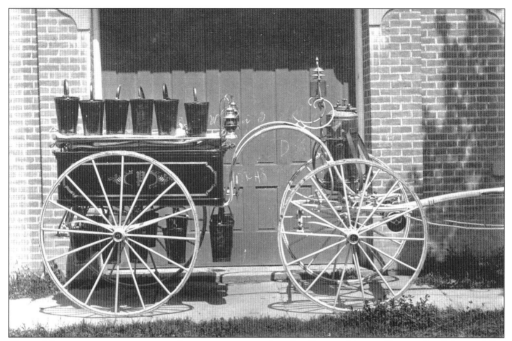

One of the most important ways that citizens served and still serve Dansville is as firefighters. The Jackson Hose and Union Hose buildings still stand, and they testify to this long, distinguished, and ongoing tradition. This is a photograph of the first fire wagon, made in Dansville in 1876. This wagon has the letter P, for Protectives. (Town of North Dansville Historian.)

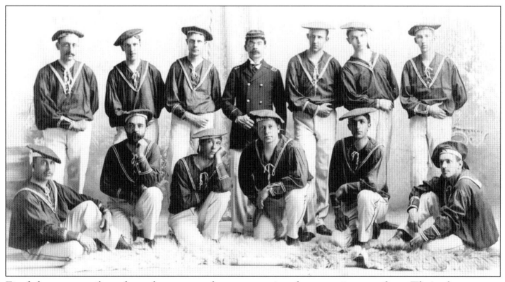

Firefighters contributed much more to the community than putting out fires. Their shows were among the social highlights of the year. Here is the minstrel group of the Union Hose. The one man not in an elaborate sailor suit wears the uniform of the Union Hose. (Town of North Dansville Historian.)

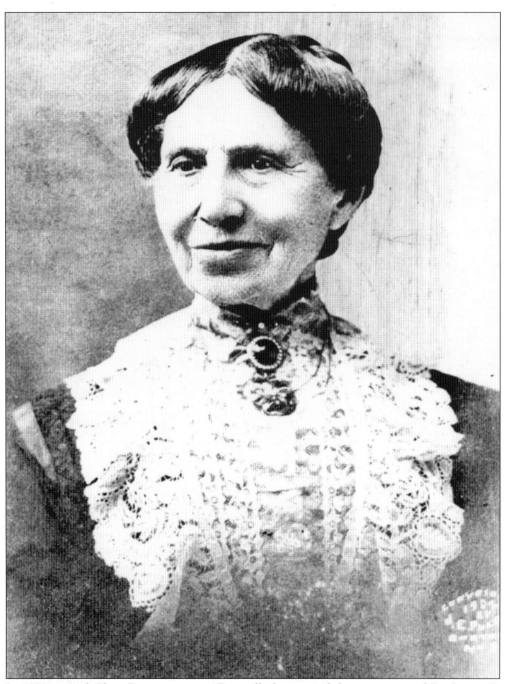

In 1876, a tired Clara Barton came to Dansville because of the reputation of Dr. James C. Jackson's spa. She stayed for a decade. While in Washington, D.C., in 1881, she founded the American Red Cross and was elected its first president. She worked with Pres. Chester A. Arthur, who had lived for several years in Livingston County. Three months later, she and a group of people in Dansville founded the first local chapter of the Red Cross. Within months, the Red Cross was helping victims of forest fires in Michigan and a bit later flood victims along the Mississippi River. (Town of North Dansville Historian.)

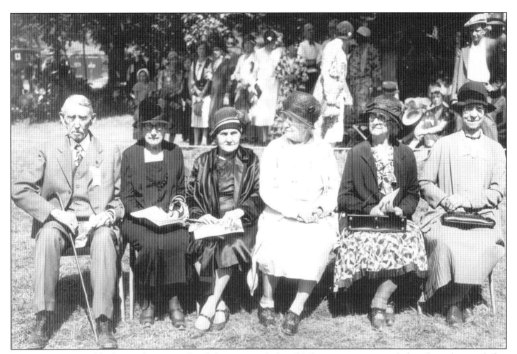

In 1931, Dansville hosted a grand celebration of the 50th anniversary of the founding of the American Red Cross. The people pictured here are the surviving charter members. (Town of North Dansville Historian.)

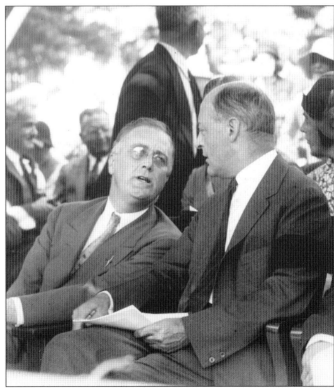

The formal 50th anniversary celebration took place in Stony Brook State Park. Two of the most distinguished guests were Gov. Franklin D. Roosevelt and former senator James W. Wadsworth Jr. of Geneseo. Later Wadsworth served eight terms in the U.S. House of Representatives. Although Roosevelt and Wadsworth were of different parties and political dispositions, they both were important in getting the country prepared for World War II. (Town of North Dansville Historian.)

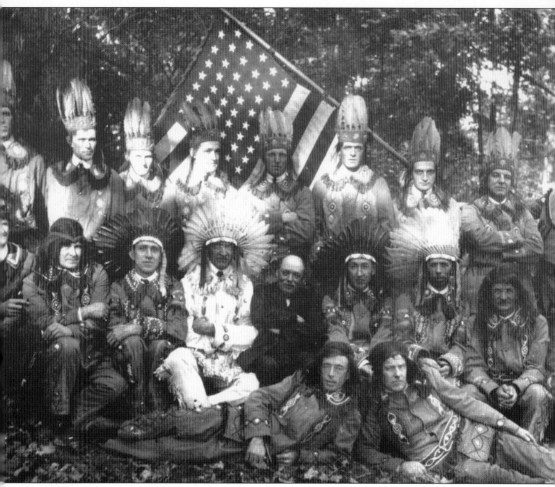

Dansville had and still has numerous civic organizations, both local (for example, the Dansville Area Historical Society) and chapters of national and international organizations such as the Lions Club. In the early 20th century, it had an active chapter of the Improved Order of Red Men, an organization that "creatively" traces its origins to the men who dressed as Native Americans at the Boston Tea Party. This was a fraternal and charitable organization and sometimes put on mock battles and elaborate pageants. (Town of North Dansville Historian.)

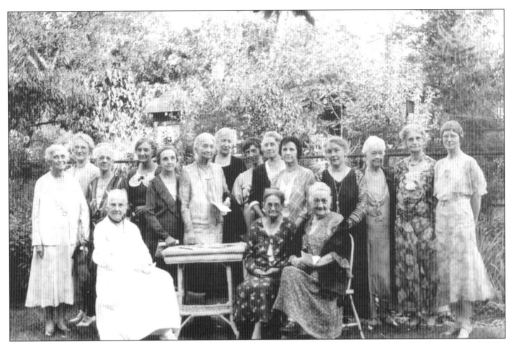

A bit more genteel than the Red Men were the members of Dansville's Shakespeare Club. Assuming that they put on productions, one wonders where they recruited for the male roles. (Town of North Dansville Historian.)

Civic organizations had several serious functions, but they also had a lot of fun. The Rotary Club in Dansville staged this comic wedding in the 1920s. Presumably the "bride" is the largest member of Rotary and the "groom" the smallest. The Rotarians referred to this skit as the Womanless Wedding. (Town of North Dansville Historian.)

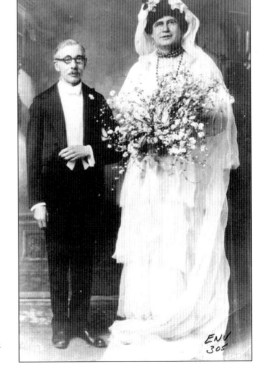

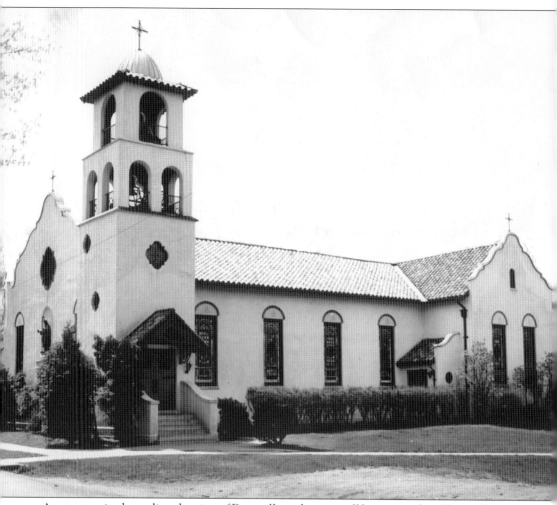

As was seen in the earliest drawing of Dansville and as can still be seen in the village of Dansville, churches are plentiful. Although most were built in the styles of churches throughout western New York, one of the most unusual church buildings in Dansville was its second Catholic church, St. Patrick's, built in the Spanish mission style. The church is still standing but currently belongs to the Assemblies of God and thus no longer has the crosses on the front, tower, and transept. (Genesee Country Express.)

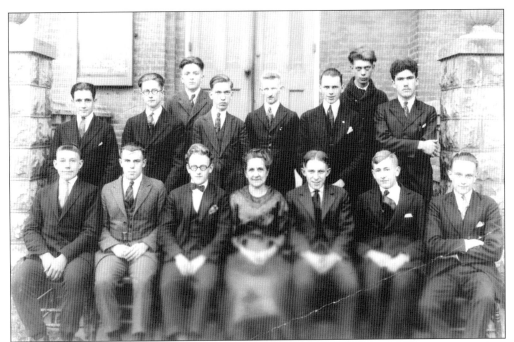

This group in front of the Methodist church may be the Sabbath School that is mentioned on the sign to the left. If so, presumably the woman in the center is the teacher. (Town of North Dansville Historian.)

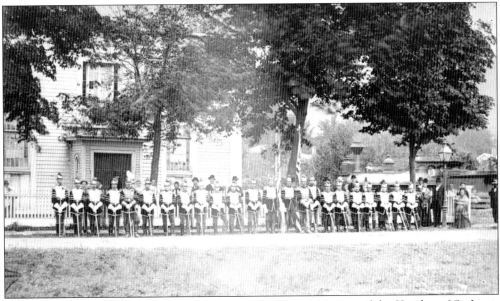

Fund-raising in today's churches is nothing new. In 1881, this group of the Knights of St. Louis traveled to Dansville from Rochester to perform and help St. Mary's Catholic Church raise funds. The building pictured is the old St. Mary's. When parishioners built a new church, they deliberately moved away from the train station, probably because of the noise. This photograph also contains one of the earliest records of Dansville's first gas streetlights. (Town of North Dansville Historian.)

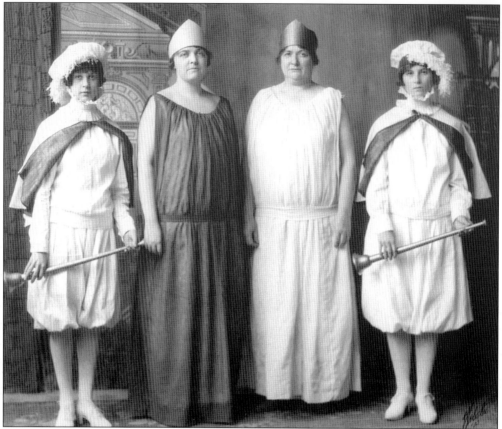

Churches, like other organizations, served many functions. In 1925, the Presbyterian church staged a pageant at the opera house to celebrate the 100th anniversary of the establishment of the village of Dansville. The two formidable women in the center represent Church Spirit and Community Spirit. When these ladies were not performing, they were schoolteachers. (Town of North Dansville Historian.)

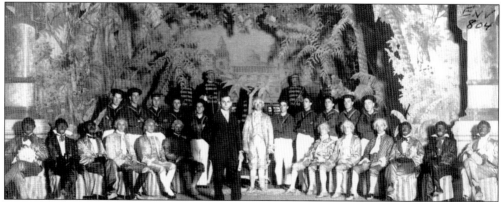

St. Mary's put on this elaborate minstrel show. It is a rather bizarre combination of a traditional blackface minstrel show, a group dressed in courtly outfits including powdered wigs, and people wearing sailor suits that they may have borrowed from the Union Hose. (Town of North Dansville Historian.)

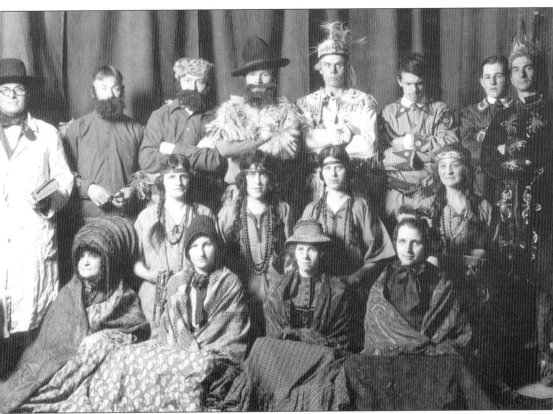

This is another part of the Presbyterians' centennial presentation. Apparently the entire history of Dansville was reenacted. This group played Native Americans and settlers. The man on the far right portrayed the great Native American chief Red Jacket. (Town of North Dansville Historian.)

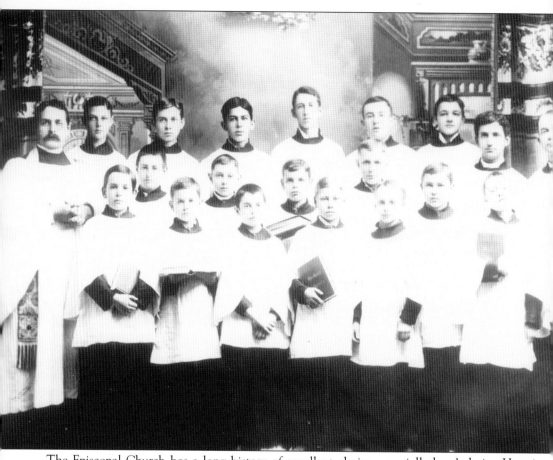

The Episcopal Church has a long history of excellent choirs, especially boys' choirs. Here is Dansville's contribution to that distinguished tradition. (Town of North Dansville Historian.)

Four
Recreation and Leisure

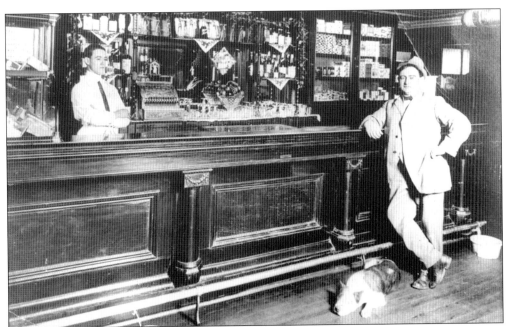

This hardly looks like the fictional Cheers because this fellow is drinking alone. However, it is an excellent photograph of a bar in Dansville about 1900. It sold both alcohol and tobacco and had spittoons and a rather relaxed dog. (Town of North Dansville Historian.)

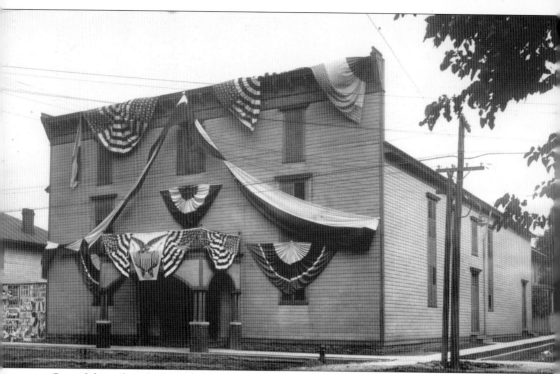

One of the cultural centers of Dansville was the opera house. Here it is bedecked with patriotic bunting. To the left is a bank of posters that describe some of the coming attractions. The opera house presented both local and traveling professional productions. (Town of North Dansville Historian.)

These two men were members of the Fearless Hook and Ladder Company. In addition to their performance at the opera house in 1910, there was an orchestra plus exhibitions of clog dancing and bag punching. (Town of North Dansville Historian.)

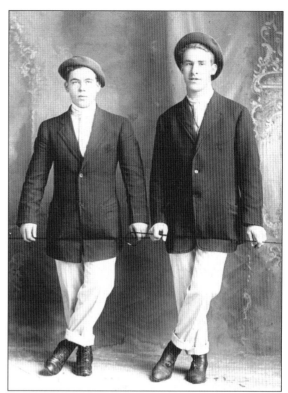

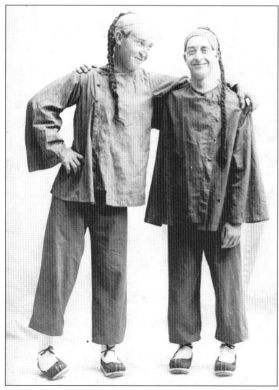

The Union House entertainment in 1896 included two members dressed as Chinese men. China at the time was a distant empire, although a few years later, American troops were sent there during the Boxer Rebellion. There were virtually no Asians in Livingston County around 1900, but today a Chinese restaurant is on Dansville's Main Street and a total of 50 self-identified Asians live in Dansville, emblematic of the changes to the ethnic makeup of the community. (Town of North Dansville Historian.)

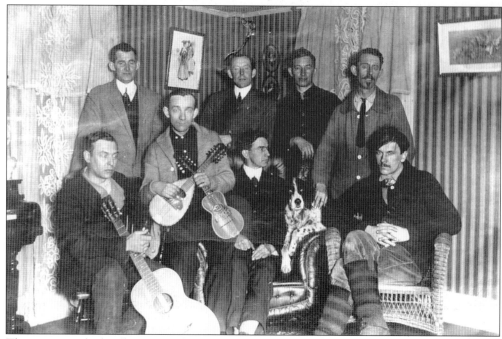

There were undoubtedly many informal musical performances, people getting together to play and sing familiar songs for their own delight. This undated photograph shows such a group, probably in the home of one of the musicians. (Town of North Dansville Historian.)

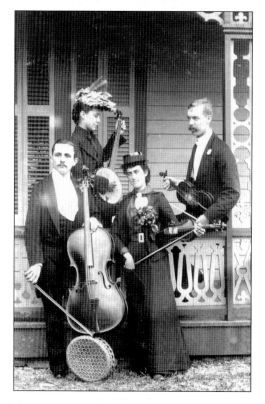

There was of course more "serious" entertainment in Dansville. This elegantly dressed string quartet probably performed in the 1890s. There is an oddity here; along with the violin, viola, and cello is a banjo. (Town of North Dansville Historian.)

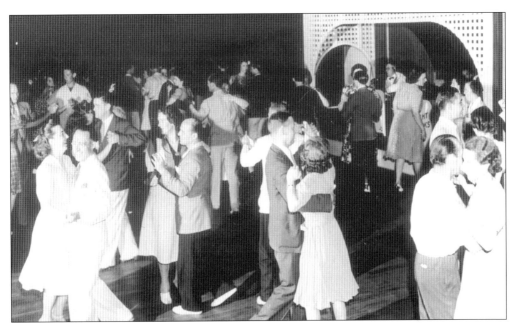

There were participatory and not just spectator public events. Here people are dancing on the roof of the Genesee Valley Manor Hotel. (Town of North Dansville Historian.)

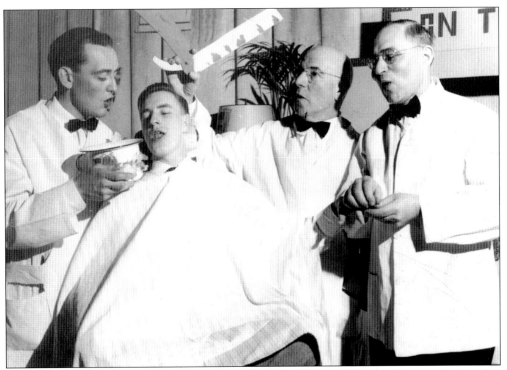

Barbershop quartets were popular throughout the United States. The close harmonies were fun to perform as men crooned about a wild Irish rose, perhaps waiting down by the old millstream. This group was performing, as members are pictured in costume and the stage prop is a giant razor. (Town of North Dansville Historian.)

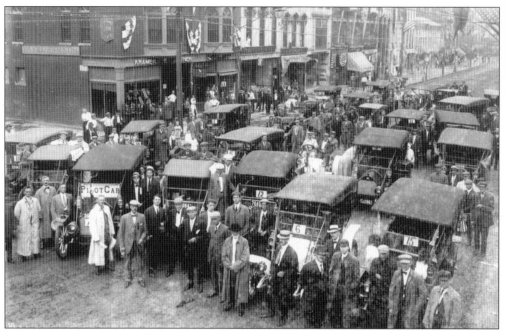

America has a continuing love affair with the automobile. As early as 1911, Dansville had a car rally that convened at the corner of Main and Ossian Streets. The pilot car led these entries on an outing to Mount Morris. Since the streets and roads were not yet paved, events like this one depended on good weather. (Livingston County Historian.)

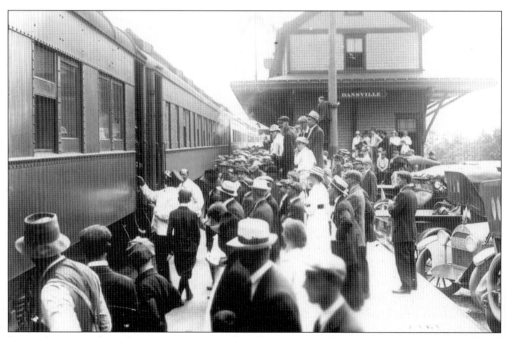

Just as the internal combustion engine introduced greater mobility for people, so had the railroad since its arrival in Dansville shortly after the Civil War. Here is a passenger train in Dansville's Lackawanna Railroad station. (Town of North Dansville Historian.)

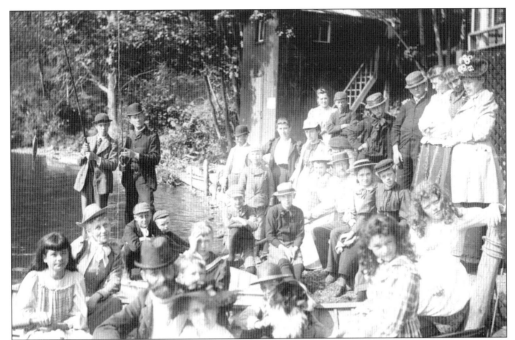

Some Dansvillians "got out of town" by heading north to Hemlock Lake, a popular resort before Rochester made it a reservoir. By modern standards, these Presbyterians on an outing from Dansville are dressed quite formally for picnicking and fishing and generally enjoying the fresh air and beautiful water. (Town of North Dansville Historian.)

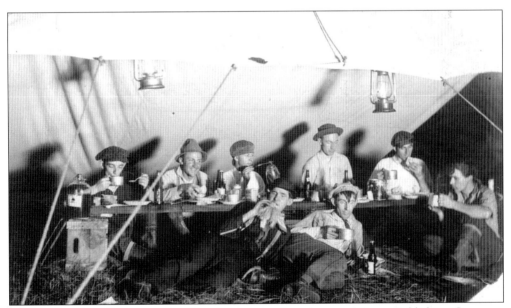

Camping in the fall was popular. Here is a group of employees of Owen Publishing Company spending a relaxed night in the wild—well, not quite. The site was near Highland Avenue, within walking distance of Main Street. For these fellows, roughing it consisted of eating and drinking some beer. The tent also has lanterns. (Town of North Dansville Historian.)

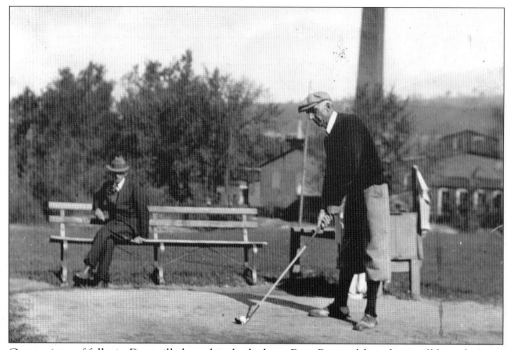

Generations of folks in Dansville have hit the links at Brae Burn, although not all have been as nattily attired as the Foster brothers. The factory in the background was the paper mill. (Town of North Dansville Historian.)

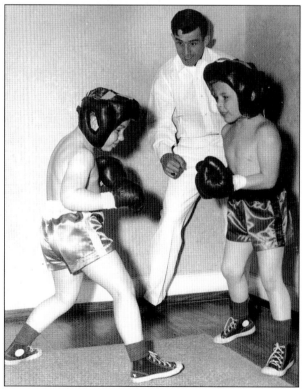

Boxing was a popular sport in Dansville. There were bouts at the Jackson Sanatorium and in public parks. In the early 1950s, Ron and Don Sylor started at a very young age. (Henrietta and Don Sylor.)

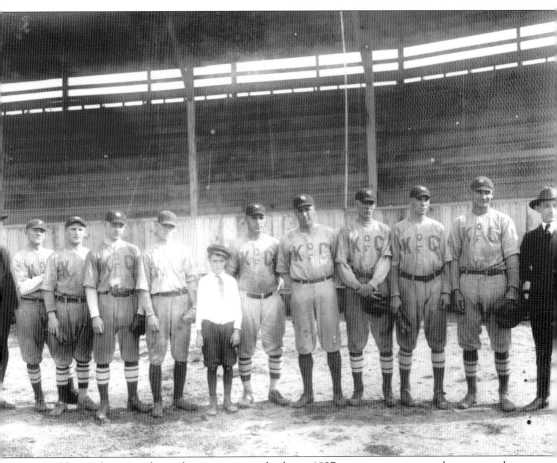

Blum Field, on the site where the airport was built in 1927, saw some vigorously contested baseball games. Typical of local teams was the Knights of Columbus team in 1920. There was no room for injuries or no-shows since there are only nine players ready to take the field. (Town of North Dansville Historian.)

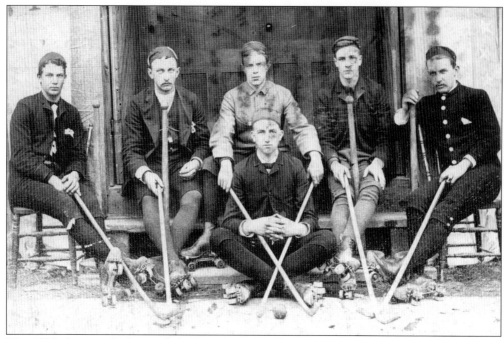

This 1885 photograph shows a hybrid sport. It is a polo team, but the players are on roller skates rather than horses. (Town of North Dansville Historian.)

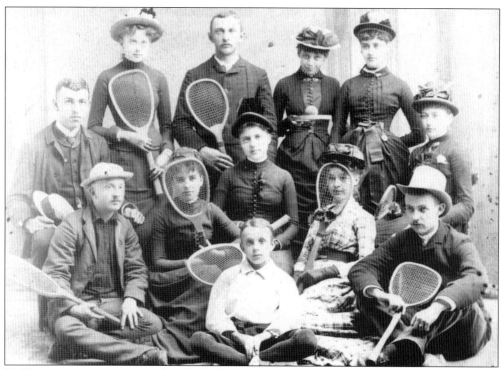

Unlike some sports, tennis was played by both men and women and by both children and adults. This group of tennis afficionados was photographed in 1880. (Town of North Dansville Historian.)

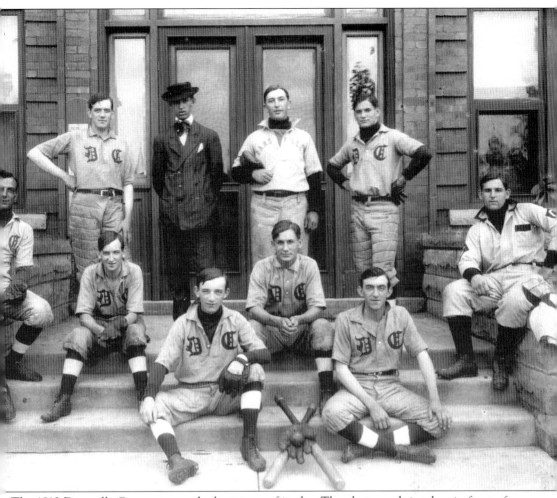

The 1912 Dansville Crescents was the best team of its day. The photograph is taken in front of the Owen Publishing Company, and presumably this team was made up of its employees. It is hard to imagine any team having a better dressed coach. (Town of North Dansville Historian.)

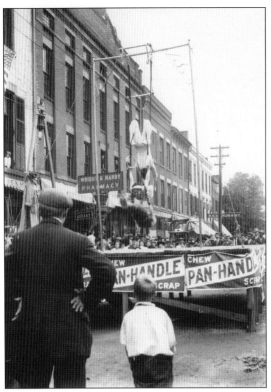

Certainly parades were a major form of entertainment, as was seen in chapter 1. This "float" contains three gymnasts on a trapeze. The advertising on it is for chewing tobacco. A hard-to-see sign under the pharmacy sign reads "Kodaks," manufactured up the road a way in Rochester. (Town of North Dansville Historian.)

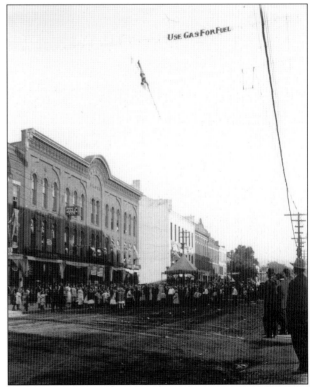

Main Street is a place of business, of course, but it is so much more. This early photograph shows a carnival complete with a bizarre high-wire act across Main Street. (Town of North Dansville Historian.)

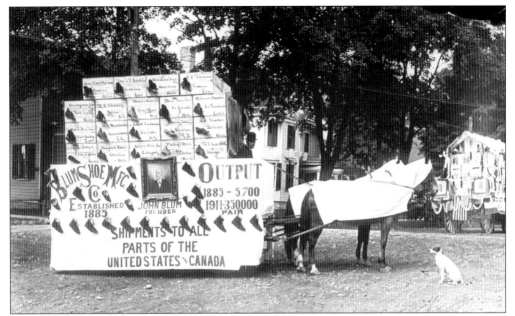

Old Home Week of 1911 included a parade with a float that advertises the locally manufactured Blum shoes. The founder's picture is prominently featured. The boxes show sample shoes and list stores throughout the United States and Canada that sold Blum's footwear. They include great cities such as San Francisco, Detroit, and Seattle as well as small towns in Montana, South Dakota, Iowa, Mississippi, and Minnesota. (Town of North Dansville Historian.)

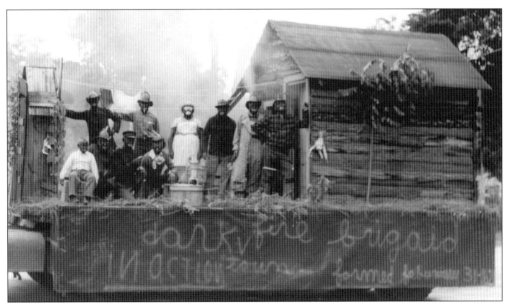

Not all of the floats were so tasteful, at least by modern standards. This one, entered by one of the volunteer fire companies, parodies black people. Firefighters are in blackface, and they are shown to be incompetent in putting out a fire. The scrawled sign deliberately misspells words such as "Brigaid," and it gives the company's founding date as "Febuwary 31." It was not until the Civil Rights Movement that such parodying was abandoned. (Town of North Dansville Historian.)

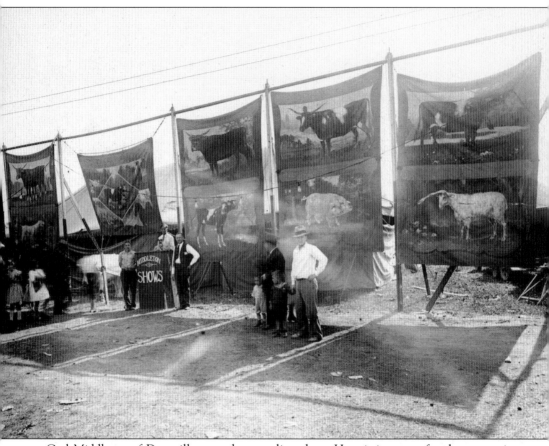

Carl Middleton of Dansville owned a traveling show. Here it is set up for the entertainment of his fellow Dansvillians. It was largely a freak show of animals. In the painted banners are a six-legged steer (to the left of the entrance), a two-headed pig (behind the man in the white shirt), and a goat with a unicorn-like horn (far right). (Town of North Dansville Historian.)

Five

HOME AND FAMILY

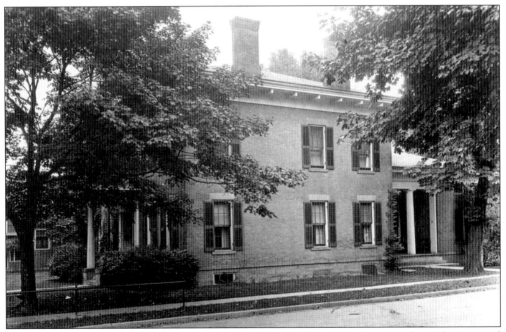

Dansville had its rich, middling, and poor residents. The early photographs of homes and families are mostly of wealthier folks because they could afford photography. Hence, a complete demographic of Dansville is not available through surviving photographs. Wealthy Dansvillians built beautiful homes, some, like this one, with multiple fireplaces and porches. (Town of North Dansville Historian.)

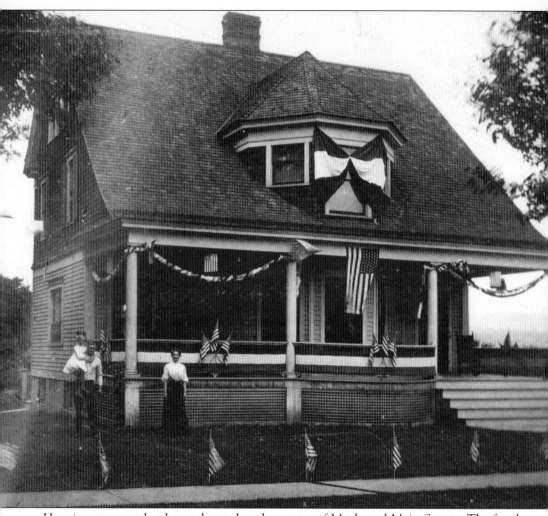

Here is a more modest home, located at the corner of Maple and Main Streets. The family, a mother, father, and daughter, chose to have the photograph taken when the house was decorated for a patriotic event. The large flag appears to have 46 stars, suggesting that this photograph was taken between 1907, when Oklahoma became the 46th state, and 1912, when New Mexico and Arizona entered the union. (Town of North Dansville Historian.)

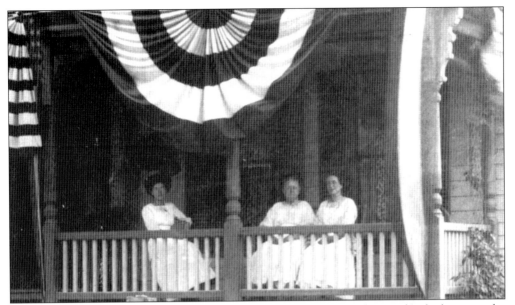

Three women, perhaps a mother and two adult daughters, sit on the porch of a home at the corner of Ossian and Spruce Streets. Although porches are not year-round gathering spots because of the weather, they are places to enjoy and to greet friends and neighbors when the weather is good. Today residents still notice every spring when porch sitting begins anew how much the children down the street have grown and how much their parents have aged. (Town of North Dansville Historian.)

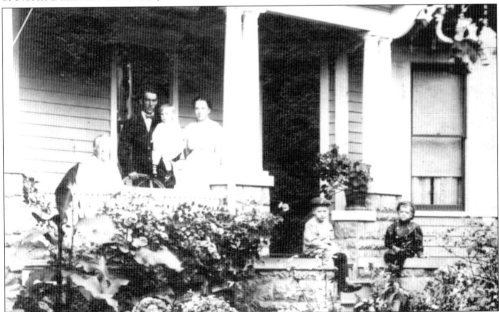

This Main Street home was the residence for a three-generation family: three children, their parents, and a grandmother. It was common for aging parents to live with their children and to die at home. As was seen in several of the photographs in chapter 2, many women worked outside the home. Grandparents were of great value to working mothers in days before professional child care facilities and labor-saving devices in the home. (Town of North Dansville Historian.)

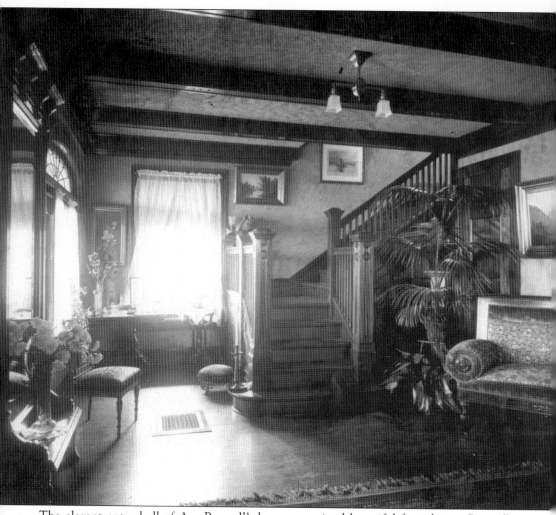

The elegant entry hall of Asa Bunnell's home contained beautiful furnishings. Bunnell was publisher of the *Dansville Advertiser* and named his house Topcol, newspaper lingo for "top of the column," meaning of highest importance. Alas, this grand house, built in 1904 at the head of Austin Street, burned 21 years later. Many precious sources for the history of Dansville were lost in that conflagration. (Town of North Dansville Historian.)

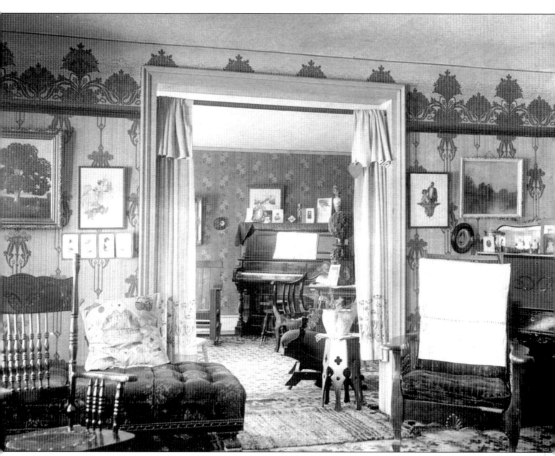

This beautiful interior was photographed about 1890. The style of wallpaper seen here and decoration with numerous small pictures were popular in the Gay Nineties. The chair on the right had an adjustable back and was for the man, while the rocking chair was for the woman of the house. At about the time this photograph was taken, the cost of pianos had dropped so that they were not just available to the super rich. Sheet music was cheap and piano lessons easily available; hence the piano was the center of entertainment in many homes. (Town of North Dansville Historian.)

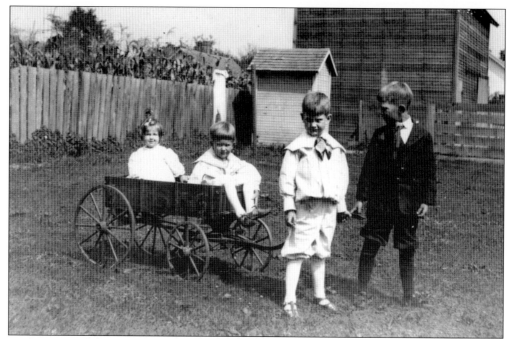

Here are the O'Grady children playing in the yard of their Perine Street home about 1912. It is unlikely that all kids had wagons such as this one, but all used outhouses like the one in the background. (Mary Jo Marks.)

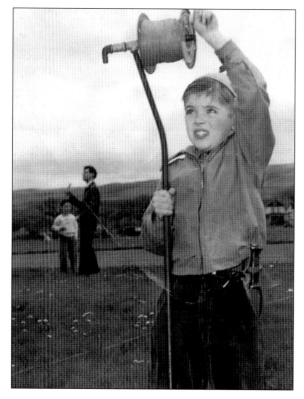

Each era has its "cool" forms of play and competition. After World War II, the Dansville Knights of Columbus sponsored a kite-flying contest. Fran Gilligan, with his elaborate, homemade winder, took a first prize in 1952 at the Dansville airport. He was ready for an emergency repair with a knife strapped to his left side. (Town of North Dansville Historian.)

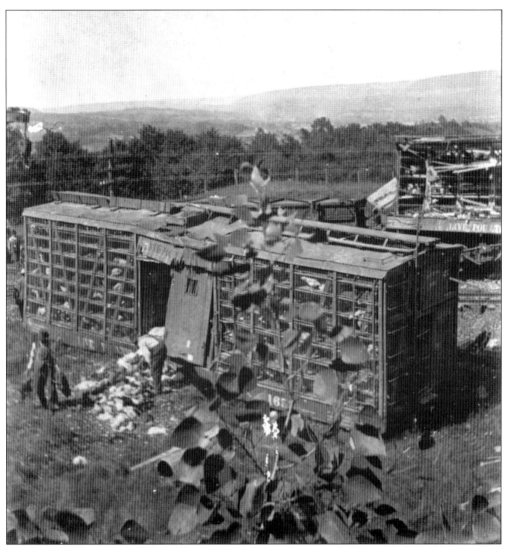

Because of the fertility of the soil, even poor Dansvillians probably ate better than the poor in large cities. This photograph shows a culinary windfall that occurred in 1920 when a 40-car train carrying live chickens to New York City derailed on East Hill, freeing thousands of chickens. For days, people captured or shot chickens around Dansville and feasted for free on food intended for folks in Manhattan. (Town of North Dansville Historian.)

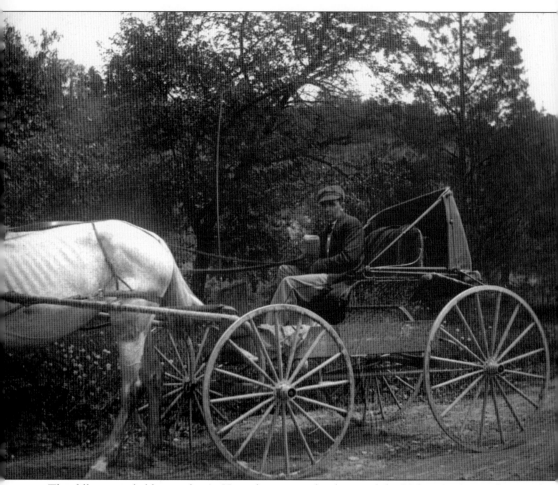
This fellow is probably a mailman. He is also a reminder that until the 20th century, people moved around town and countryside either by foot or by horse. (Town of North Dansville Historian.)

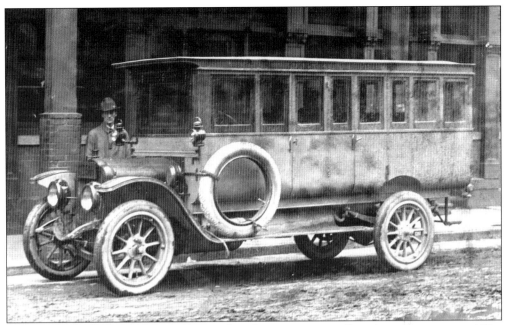

At the beginning of the century, new modes of transportation allowed people greater mobility to make trips to neighboring towns. This is the bus that ran from Dansville to Hornell in 1914. (Town of North Dansville Historian.)

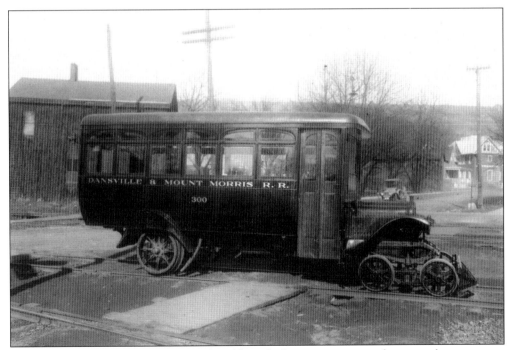

The Dansville and Mount Morris Railroad launched passenger service between the two towns in 1917, using what looks like a half railroad car and half bus. The trip took 40 minutes, and the car had a capacity of 24 passengers. (Town of North Dansville Historian.)

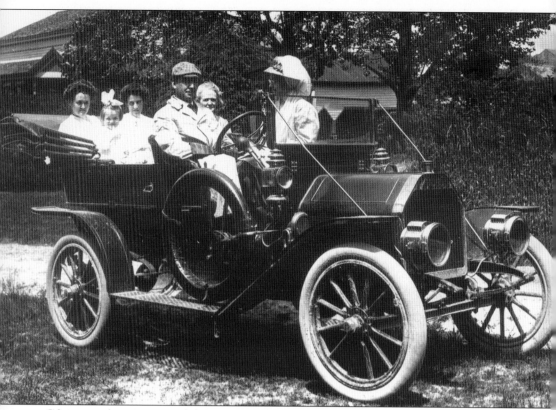

Of course, the greatest mobility came with the automobile. Photographs on pages 41 and 44 show a mass of automobiles in downtown Dansville. The main cause of the explosion of cars was the introduction of Henry Ford's Model T in 1908, allowing middle-class people to own cars. This three-generation family from Dansville is shown going out for a drive. (Town of North Dansville Historian.)

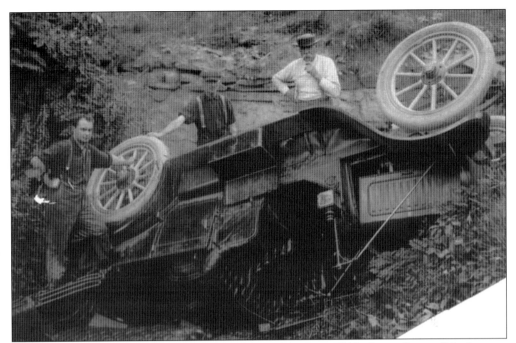

Automobiles created new dangers. This photograph from 1910 shows Dansville's first car accident. Alas, this was a harbinger of things to come even after cars became much safer to ride in. (Town of North Dansville Historian.)

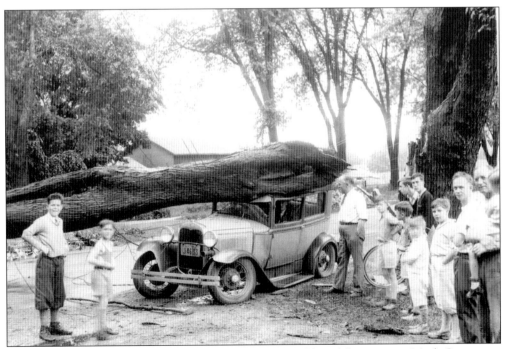

During a 1933 windstorm, Lynn Pickard's car was destroyed by a falling tree on Maple Street near Main Street. Fortunately no one was in the car at the time. (Town of North Dansville Historian.)

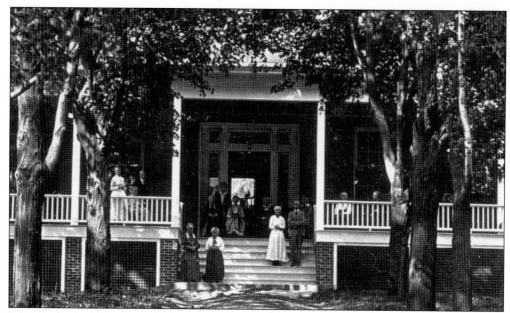

In 1919, the building that originally had been a seminary (school for postsecondary education) and later Dansville's first hospital opened as the King's Daughters' Home, a nondenominational place for elderly women to live. It was part of a nationwide group of such homes. Here some of the residents enjoy the weather and some good conversation. There appear to be male guests. Today the facility also accepts men and is known as the King's Daughters' and Sons' Home. (Town of North Dansville Historian.)

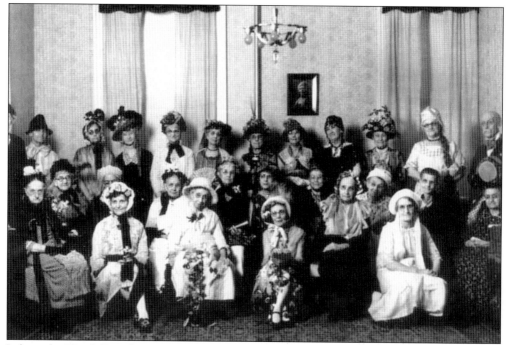

Life at the King's Daughters' Home included special events such as this one in 1929. (King's Daughters' and Sons' Home.)

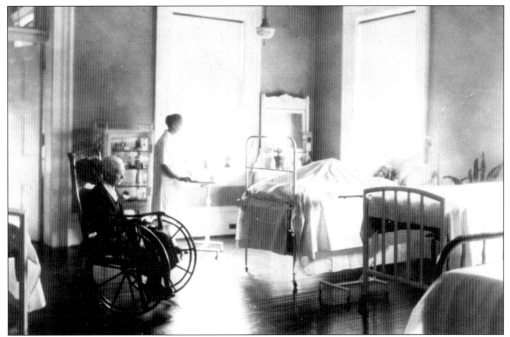

King's Daughters' Home provided necessary medical care for residents. In this photograph from 1920, a nurse attends a bedridden patient while a resident in a wheelchair looks on. (King's Daughters' and Sons' Home.)

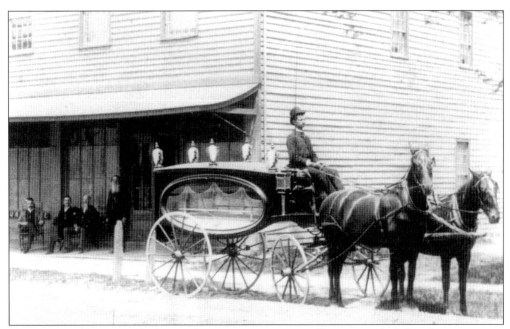

Life ends for all of us. In the late 19th century, many Dansvillians were paid their last respects as this horse-drawn hearse took the body from the mortuary at the corner of Main and Chestnut Streets to the cemetery. (Town of North Dansville Historian.)

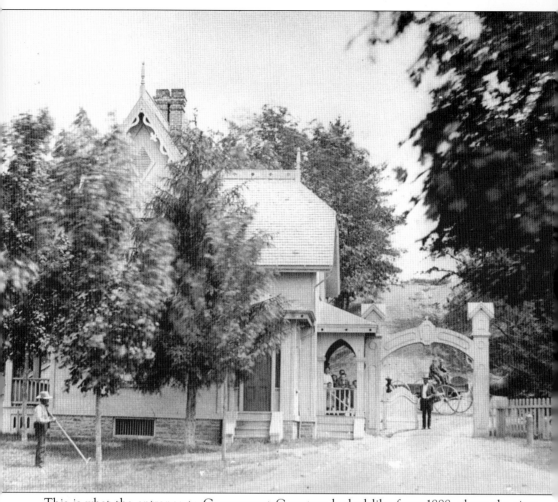

This is what the entrance to Greenmount Cemetery looked like from 1888, about the time this photograph was taken, until granite pillars were erected in 1915. (Town of North Dansville Historian.)

Six
SCHOOL DAYS

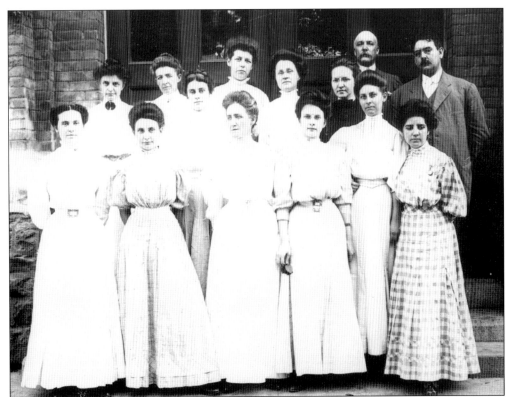

Education is the principal engine of social and economic change in America. In 1907, the teachers in Dansville were virtually all female, but the administration was in the hands of the men in the right rear. (Town of North Dansville Historian.)

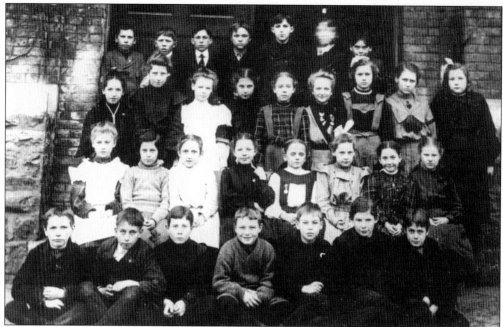

This is the fifth grade in Dansville Elementary School in 1906. Several students, especially the girls, wear clothes that reflect the German origins of the town. In the next photograph, taken 12 years later, there are no German-looking outfits because the United States was at war with Germany. (Town of North Dansville Historian.)

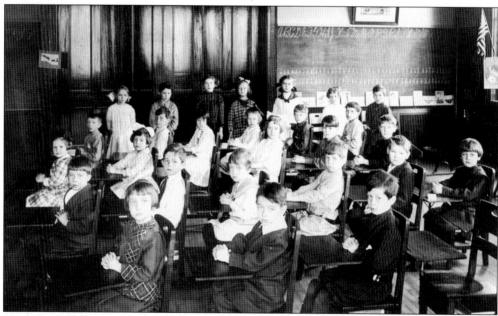

This photograph was taken in Dansville Elementary School in 1918. School was much more formal at that time than now. On the blackboard, one can see the letters of the alphabet and below them a long series of mathematical statements beginning with 1 + 1 = 2. On the left doorjamb is a drawing of Aesop's fable of the tortoise and the hare. Some of these children may have seen their fathers march off to World War I. (Town of North Dansville Historian.)

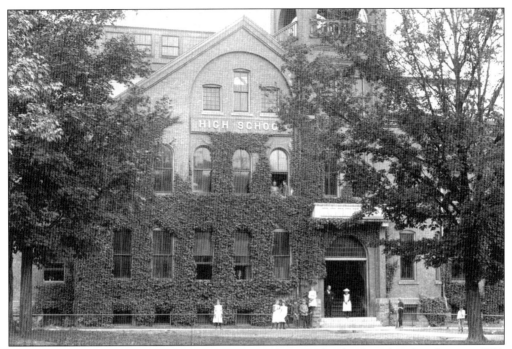

The high school was dedicated in 1888. Later it served as a grade school until its demolition in 1956. The bell from the tower is preserved in the new high school. (Town of North Dansville Historian.)

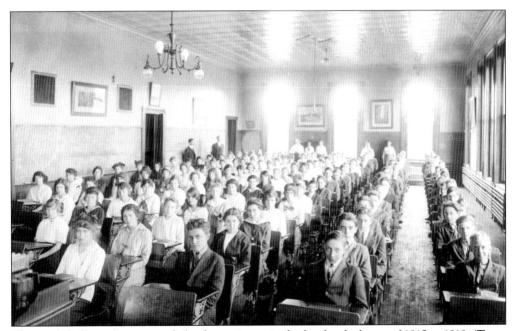

This study hall was large enough for the entire senior high school, classes of 1915 to 1918. (Town of North Dansville Historian.)

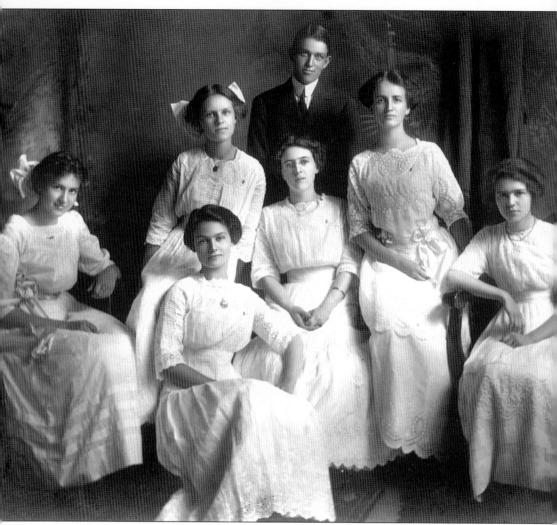

Here is the graduating class of 1911. It is surprisingly small given the size of the student body in the preceding photograph. One might expect to see about 30 graduates. However, a high school diploma was not needed to work on the family farm or to get a job in some of the industries in Dansville. The one male graduate was, unsurprisingly, class president. (Town of North Dansville Historian.)

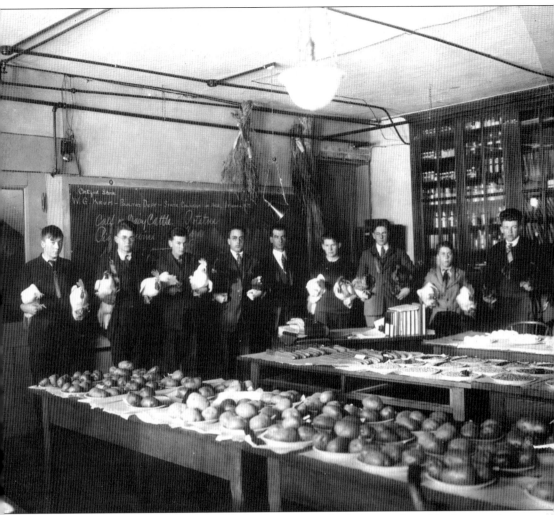

The agriculture class of 1923 must have been holding a special exhibition when this photograph was taken. There are potatoes, beans, corn, and eggs on the table, and each student holds at least one live chicken. On the blackboard is written the name of a professor at the New York College of Agriculture in Ithaca, a part of Cornell University. (Town of North Dansville Historian.)

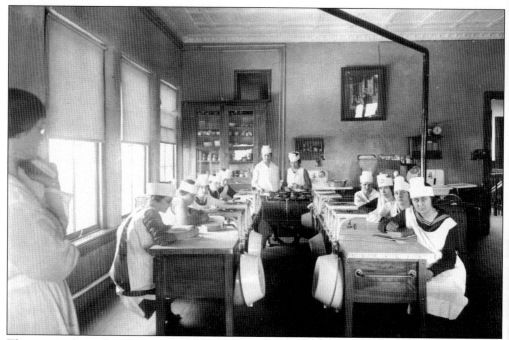

This is a cooking class from around 1920. There are several gas burners and lots of pots for the students. (Town of North Dansville Historian.)

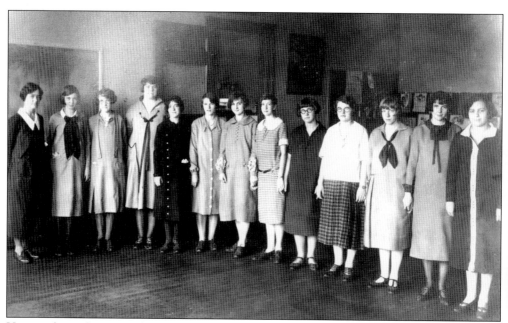

Homemaking classes involved sewing as well as cooking. About 1924, the students display the fashions they had created. (Town of North Dansville Historian.)

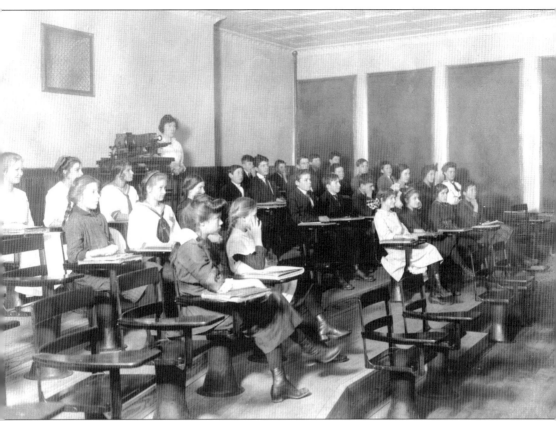

New technology changed the way students learned. This 1914 photograph shows a redesigned room in the high school to provide for the maximum effectiveness of the stereopticon, a device that allowed for the projection of images. Chiefly, this device enhanced social studies classes, for students could see the places they were studying. (Town of North Dansville Historian.)

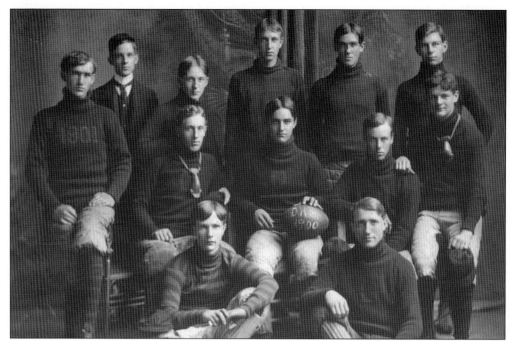

Of course, school was hardly all study and no play. This is the Dansville High School football team for the fall of 1900, as the inscription on the ball indicates. The player on the far left wears a sweater with the year 1901 across his chest. Especially noticeable is the lack of padding, although the "necklaces" on some of the players are noseguards. Presumably the boy wearing a tie is a manager or mascot. It is interesting that the backdrop used by the photographer is the same as seen in many formal family photographs. (Town of North Dansville Historian.)

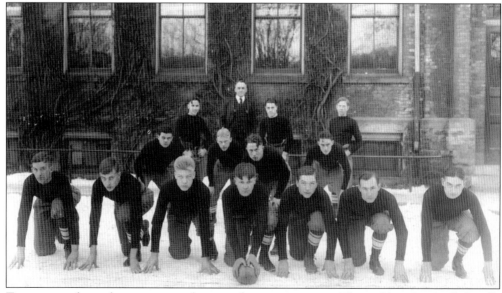

Twenty years later, there are more players and more equipment. The padding was made locally by the Blum Shoe Manufacturing Company, and cleats were simply added to a regular pair of shoes. Hopefully, given the snowy field, this photograph was taken after the season ended. (Town of North Dansville Historian.)

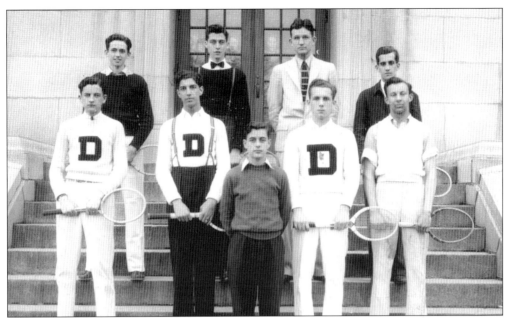

Several members of the 1936 Dansville tennis team sport letter sweaters, qualifying each of them as a BMOC (big man on campus). (Town of North Dansville Historian.)

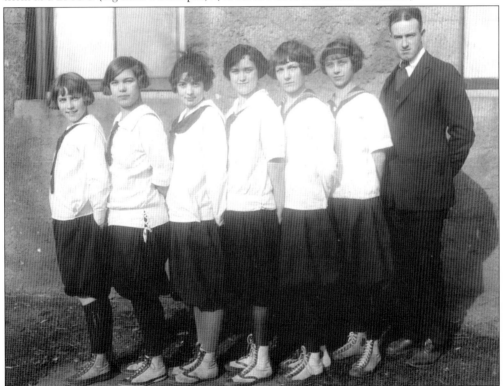

Girls' athletics were prominent in the early part of the 20th century only to decline before their revival and expansion beginning in the 1960s. This is the 1924 girls' basketball team. The players wear very impressive high-top sports shoes. (Town of North Dansville Historian.)

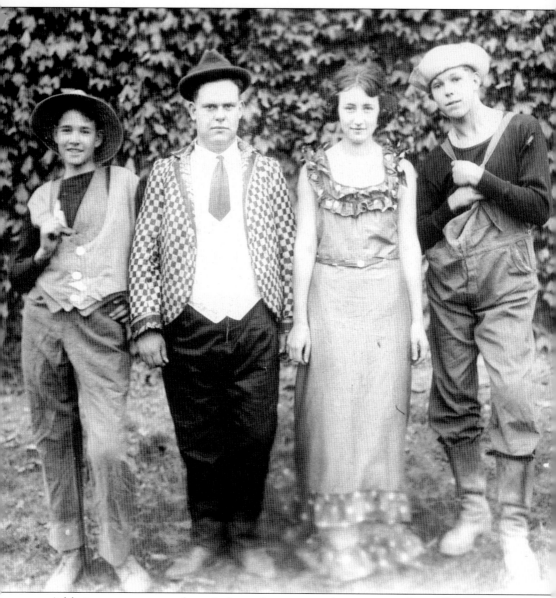
Athletic teams were not the only form of extracurricular activity at Dansville High School, as illustrated by this 1924 photograph of students in their costumes for a theatrical production. (Town of North Dansville Historian.)

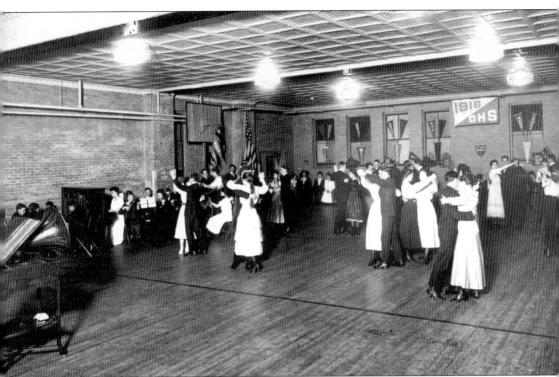

This is a formal dance in the Dansville High School gymnasium in 1916. The pennants in the windows probably indicate places that seniors or recent graduates continued their education. The two in the left window are Yale and Geneseo. While there is a small orchestra to the left, at the extreme left is a Victrola; apparently the day of the disc jockey had already arrived in Dansville! (Town of North Dansville Historian.)

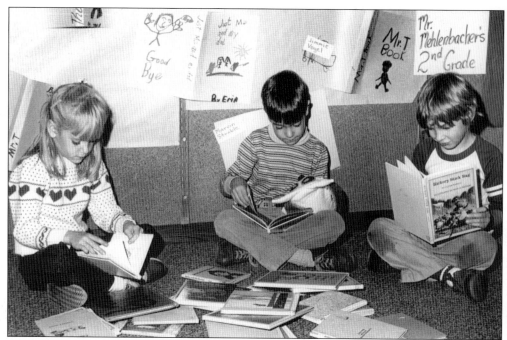

School has certainly changed since the early part of the 20th century. It is much less formal. For instance, in this 1984 photograph, children, casually and comfortably dressed, do some of their reading while sitting on the floor. (Genesee Country Express.)

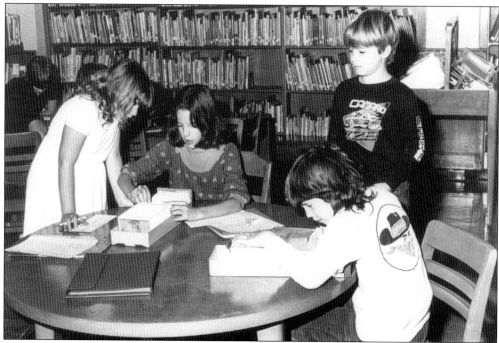

These Dansville students are learning to do research in 1984. Within a generation, research methods require a computer rather than a card catalog. The value of the books that these students are looking for, however, remains the same. (Genesee Country Express.)

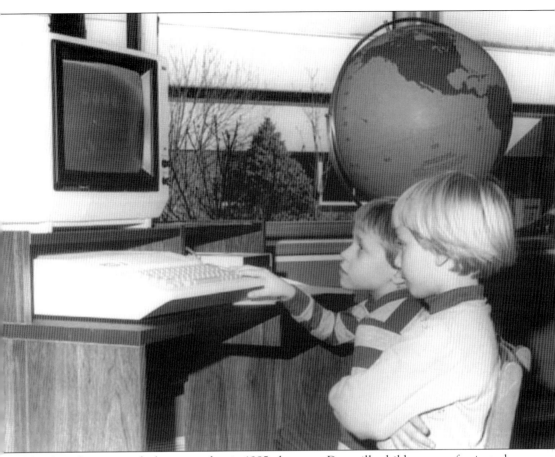

Globes have been around a long time, but in 1985, these two Dansville children seem fascinated by this new gadget called a computer. They may be wondering if it is just a fad or if it will last. (Genesee Country Express.)

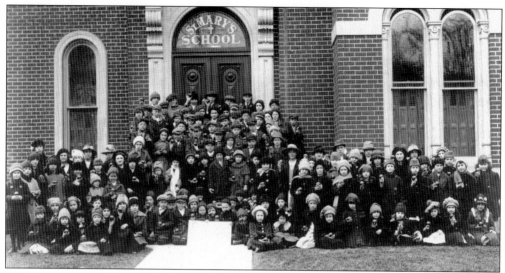

In addition to its public schools, Dansville once had two Catholic schools and still has St. Mary's. In this early photograph, each child at St. Mary's displays an orange, and the sign proclaims Orange Day. The fruit must have just arrived by train. (Town of North Dansville Historian.)

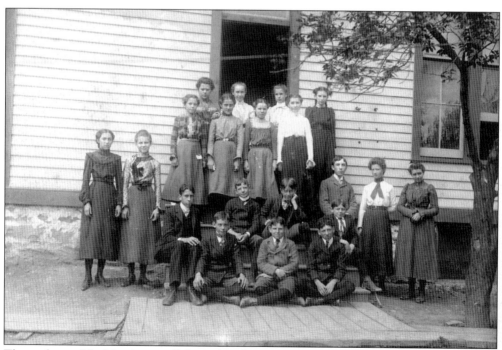

The students of St. Mary's are well dressed as they pose for this photograph. Long skirts were no doubt required for the girls, while most boys preferred stylish short pants with knee stockings. (Town of North Dansville Historian.)

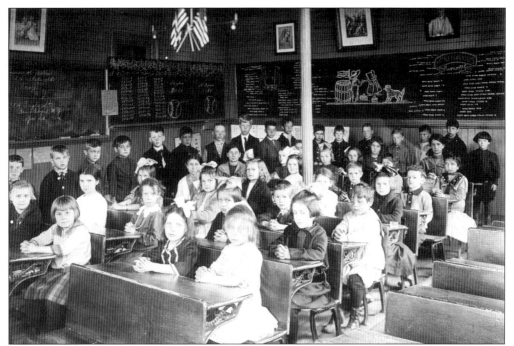

This 1914 photograph of the students of St. Mary's tells the story of Catholics in America at that time. There are many specifically Catholic elements seen here, for instance the picture in the upper right of Pope Pius X, who died later that year. The blackboard beneath Pius X has "Meritorious" written at the top in large letters. Catholics often had to "prove" that they were true Americans because they also pledged loyalty to an authority outside the United States. Hence, there are two American flags and a patriotic drawing on the blackboard. The paper posted between the two blackboards on the left is a map of Livingston County. (Town of North Dansville Historian.)

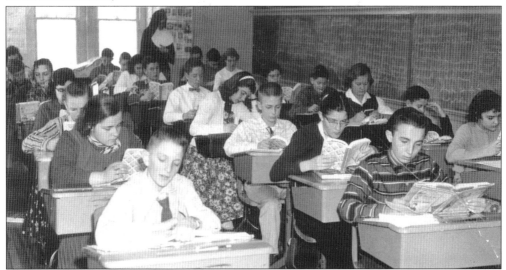

By mid-century, the old desks at St. Mary's have been replaced, and the dress is more varied and somewhat more casual. In the back of the room, the teacher—a nun—is a reminder of differences between public and parochial schools. (Town of North Dansville Historian.)

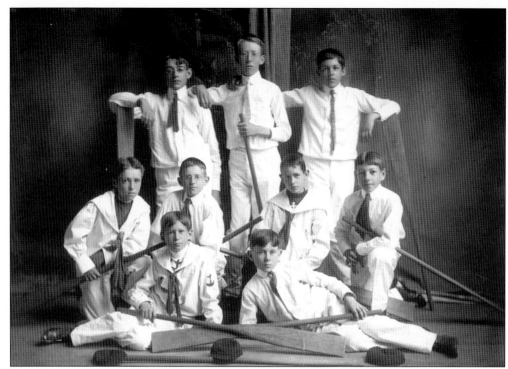

These boys who graduated from St. Mary's in 1904 put on a show called the Sailor's Oar Drill. The girls presented Prisoner's Prayer, and there was a comedy entitled Dr. Cure-all. Commencement ceremonies were clearly an elaborate event. (Town of North Dansville Historian.)

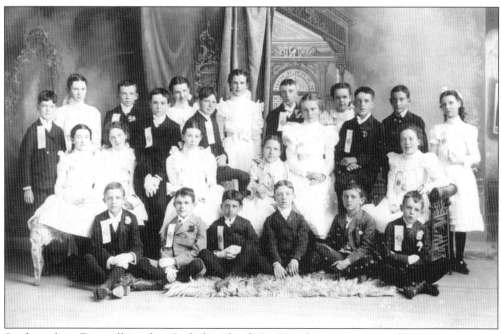

Students from Dansville's other Catholic school, St. Patrick's, are wearing ribbons containing a holy picture. Some even sport flowers. (Town of North Dansville Historian.)

Seven
THE SPA ON EAST HILL

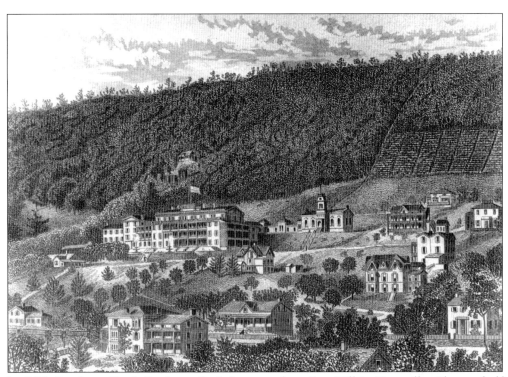

In 1798, Breakout Creek "broke out" of the ground on East Hill in Dansville. About a half century later, it became the site of Dansville Water Cures; and in 1858, Dr. James C. Jackson built Our Home on the Hillside. For more than a century, this location was a center for health. Seen in this old drawing is Our Home on the Hillside, which burned in 1882. (Town of North Dansville Historian.)

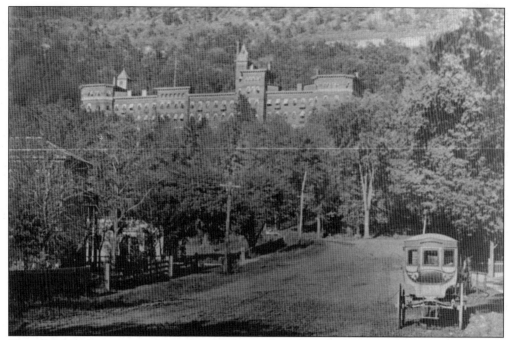

The new and elegant sanatorium that Dr. James C. Jackson built in 1883 dominates East Hill even today, although it has not been occupied since 1971. In this 1900 photograph taken from William Street is a horse-drawn bus that took folks from downtown Dansville and the Lackawanna train station to the sanatorium. (Town of North Dansville Historian.)

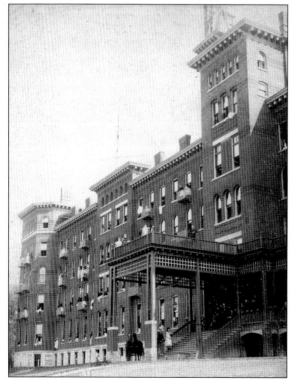

Arriving at the spa was an impressive experience. On a nice day, lots of folks watched to greet visitors. In this photograph, someone has just arrived in a horse-drawn cart. The high middle step suggests an easy way for those arriving by bus to start their climb into the facility. (Town of North Dansville Historian.)

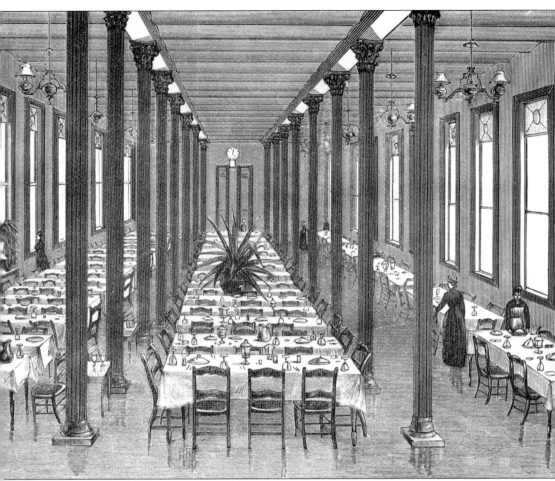
And what a facility it was. This drawing shows the elegant dining room. It is no wonder that visitors came from far and wide to enjoy the healthy environment and the stylish surroundings. (Mary Jo Marks.)

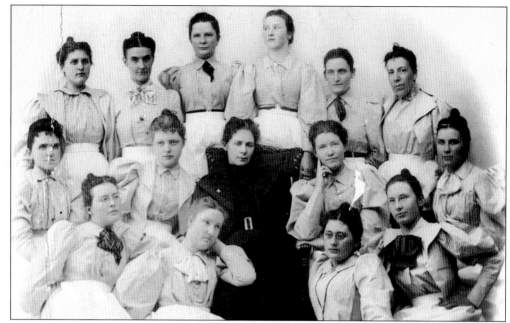

Since the focus was on water treatment, or hydropathy, there was a need for a large staff of bath attendants, shown here with their supervisor in the dark dress. Dr. James C. Jackson had himself been cured by hydropathy as a young man, and this led him to the study of medicine and his decision to create the sanatorium. This photograph was taken just before 1900. (Town of North Dansville Historian.)

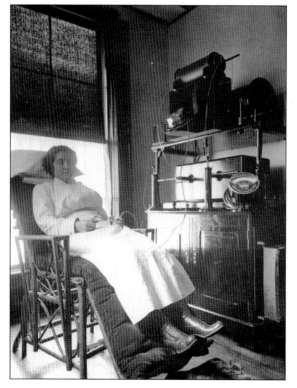

The sanatorium became far more than a place for treatment by water. Dietary considerations were central, and dry cereal was invented here under the name of Granula. Various treatments, some quite experimental, were employed, using the latest technology. Here electrical treatment is being used to improve circulation. (Town of Sparta Historian.)

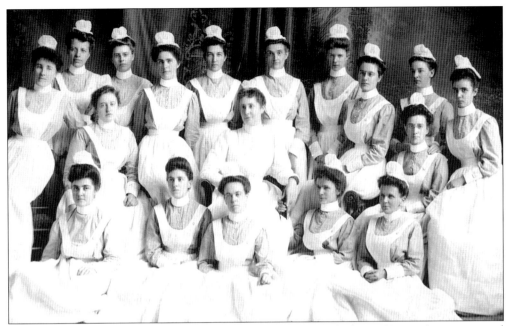

Those who came to the sanatorium received a good deal of individual care. Hence, there was a need for numerous nurses and consequently the training of nurses. In 1904, these women became the first graduates of the school of nursing at the sanatorium. (Town of North Dansville Historian.)

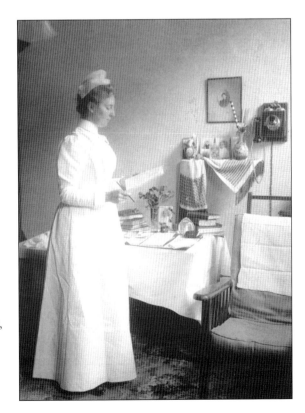

The head nurse, Mrs. Allsdorf, is shown at her station. It includes charts, books, and a telephone but also some family pictures and fresh flowers from Dr. James C. Jackson's nurseries. (Dr. Ted Jackson and the SUNY Geneseo Library.)

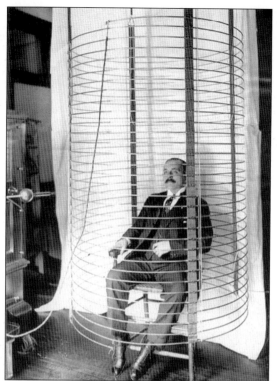

Dr. Roswell Park of Buffalo demonstrates a machine designed for cancer treatment. Park was a widely known pioneer in this field, and the famous cancer treatment center in Buffalo still bears his name today. (Noyes Memorial Hospital.)

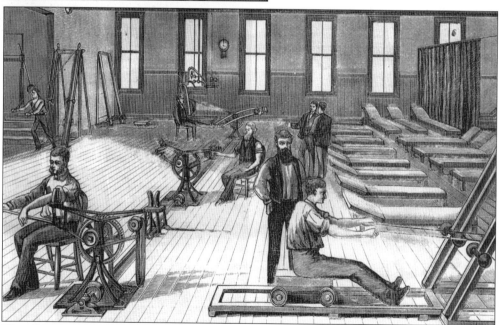

This 1884 drawing shows a new method of exercise and massage in use at the sanatorium. This section of the spa was called the Swedish Movement Department. Hartvig Nissen brought this form of massage and exercise to the United States in 1883 but did not publish his book about the Swedish Movement until 1889. The Jackson Sanatorium must have been one of the first places in the United States to offer it. (Town of Sparta Historian.)

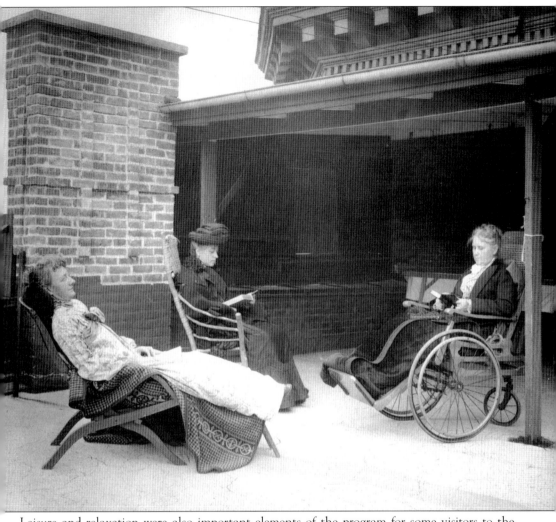

Leisure and relaxation were also important elements of the program for some visitors to the sanatorium. On good days, people could enjoy being outdoors on the spa's roof. (Dr. Ted Jackson and the SUNY Geneseo Library.)

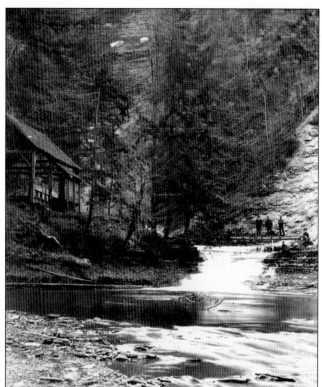

Adjacent to the sanatorium was the lovely stream that flows down East Hill. On the left is the pavilion, which was later replaced by a swimming pool. There is a footbridge across the falls at the top with several well-dressed men posing on it and a woman sitting to its right. (Town of North Dansville Historian.)

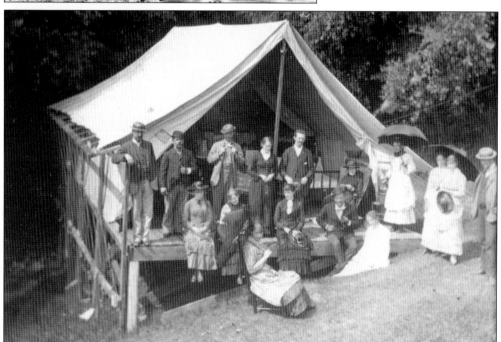

For some of the more vigorous visitors, there was a kind of genteel camping available. The tents are erected on wooden platforms, and it is clear that the campers are hardly roughing it. (Town of North Dansville Historian.)

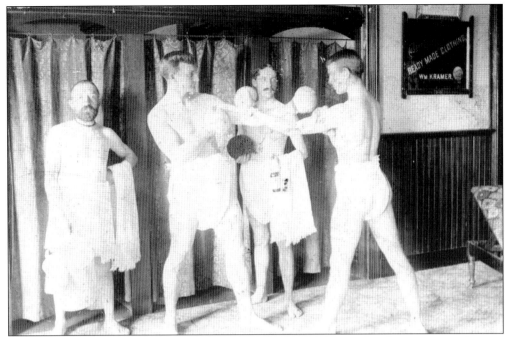

The sanatorium also provided more vigorous activities, as seen in this dressing room for men engaged in the gentlemanly sport of boxing. (Town of North Dansville Historian.)

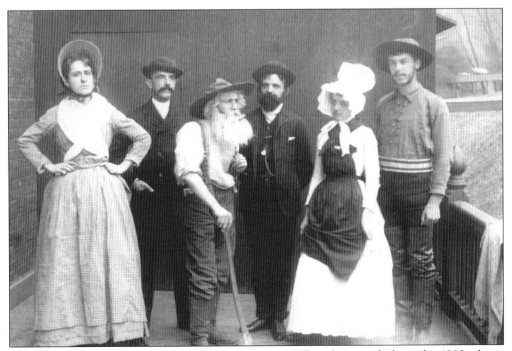

There were also cultural activities at the sanatorium. This photograph from the 1890s shows some sort of theatrical cast. To the right is a member of the Jackson family. (Town of North Dansville Historian.)

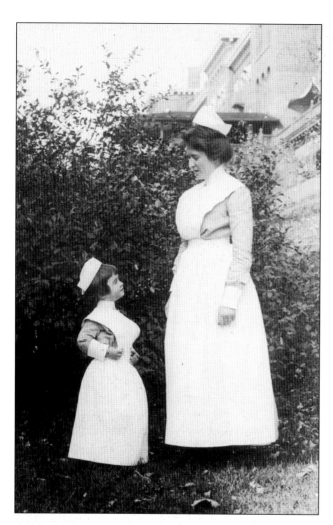

Agnes O'Grady's father was a doctor at the sanatorium. She came up to her father's place of employment to visit and perhaps even to entertain the guests. In fact, as seen here, she had her own nurse's dress. Given that the clientele consisted of adults, having lovely children around must have been a joy for them. (Mary Jo Marks.)

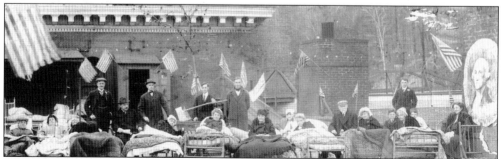

On February 22, 1910, some of the hearty (or foolhardy) residents attended a rooftop party to celebrate Pres. George Washington's 178th birthday. A large image of President Washington can be seen on the far right, and numerous 46-star flags provide a patriotic, if frosty, setting for this party. (Town of North Dansville Historian.)

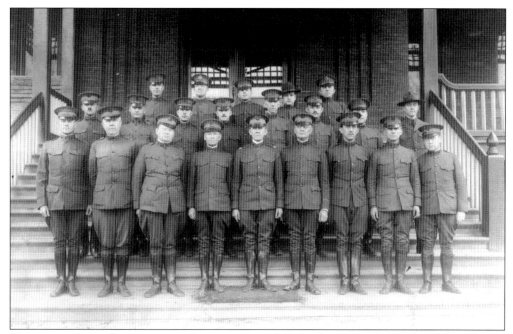

Changes in medical treatment at the beginning of the 20th century led to the Jackson family declaring bankruptcy in 1914. However, the facility took on a new task—care for veterans of World War I with psychiatric problems. This photograph shows a group of veterans who recuperated at the sanatorium. (Town of North Dansville Historian.)

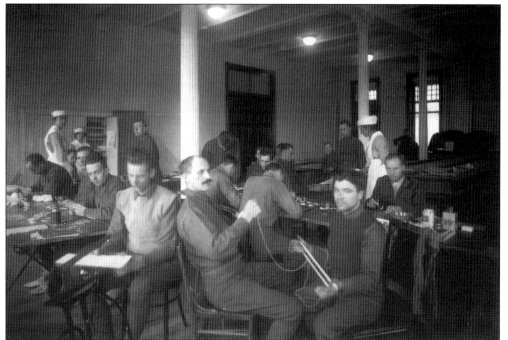

This picture gives a rare inside glimpse at some of the soldiers receiving what would today probably be considered occupational therapy. They are attended to by several staff members. (Town of North Dansville Historian.)

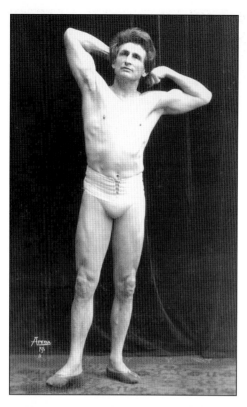

In 1929, a well-known and flamboyant proponent of physical culture, Bernarr MacFadden, bought the spa and turned it into the Physical Culture Hotel. After MacFadden's death, it was renamed Bernarr MacFadden's Castle on the Hill. It remained in business until 1971. This photograph makes clear that MacFadden was a proponent of minimal clothing and "going natural." (Henrietta and Don Sylor.)

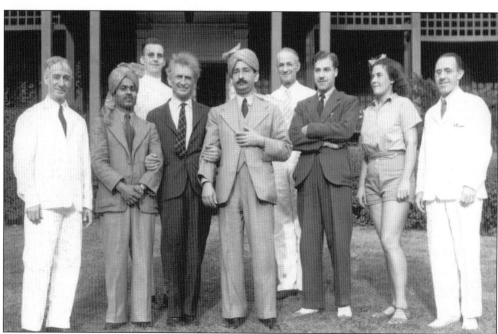

The Castle on the Hill had an international reputation. In 1940, MacFadden (fourth from the left) welcomed two men from the Punjab in India and one from Australia (dark suit, arms crossed). The others are members of the staff of the Castle on the Hill. (Town of North Dansville Historian.)

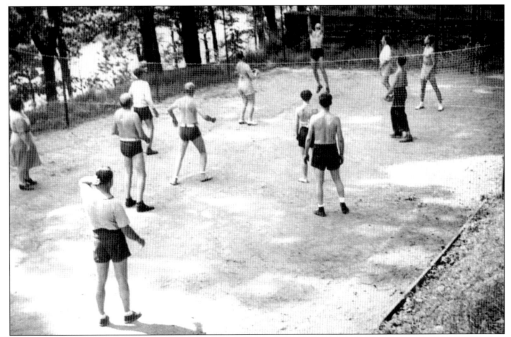

There were always physical activities at the Castle on the Hill. Here are some scantily clad men by the standards of the day engaging in a game of volleyball. One of Bernarr MacFadden's mottos was "weakness is a crime; don't be a criminal." (Town of North Dansville Historian.)

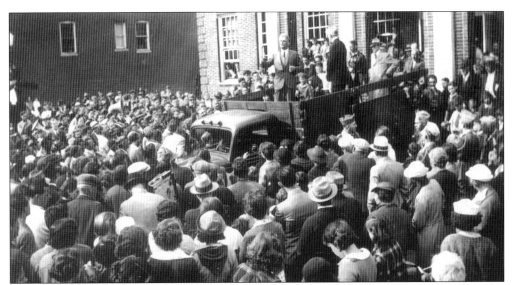

MacFadden was a showman, for example parachuting from a plane on his 81st birthday. He also sponsored bizarre events, including the so-called Cracked Wheat Derby. In 1936, 74 hikers left New York City for the 13-day, 389-mile hike to Dansville, feasting along the way on cracked wheat. Here MacFadden and townspeople greet the 53 who made it in front of the Dansville Post Office. (Town of North Dansville Historian.)

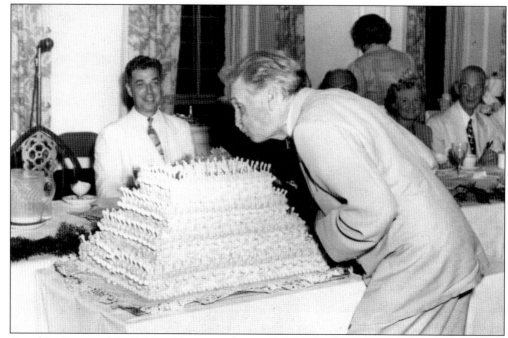

An older Bernarr MacFadden blows out the candles on his birthday cake. Presumably each candle does not stand for a year of his life, or he could have come over with the Pilgrims or perhaps even Columbus. (Town of North Dansville Historian.)

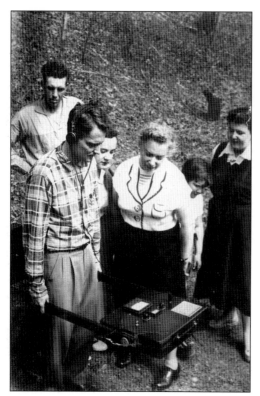

MacFadden died in 1955, leaving behind rumors that he had buried treasure on the grounds of the Castle on the Hill. Some folks brought the latest technology to try to find it—unsuccessfully, of course. Interestingly, as the Castle on the Hill was closing in 1971, a new hospital, Noyes Memorial, was in the final stages of construction. It has carried on Dansville's legacy of health care that began a century and a half ago on East Hill. (Town of North Dansville Historian.)

Eight
THE SURROUNDING TOWNS OF OSSIAN, SPARTA, AND WEST SPARTA

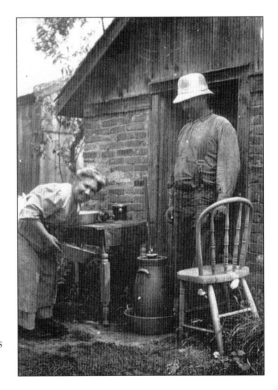

The village of Dansville is almost coterminous with the town of North Dansville. The Livingston County towns that border North Dansville are rural and have only small hamlets. An examination of them shows the overall rural nature of southern Livingston County. In this photograph, the Swartz family of the town of Sparta illustrates that life on the farm was rugged. Mrs. Swartz has just churned some butter. (Town of Sparta Historian.)

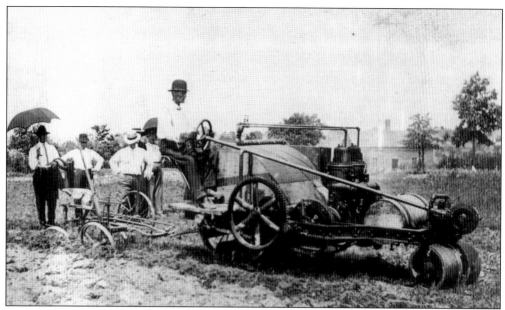

In Sparta, C. R. Traxler plowed using a crude oil traction engine for power about 1910. His hat perhaps suggests that this is some sort of demonstration, and the man with the umbrella indicates that the weather is hot. (Town of Sparta Historian.)

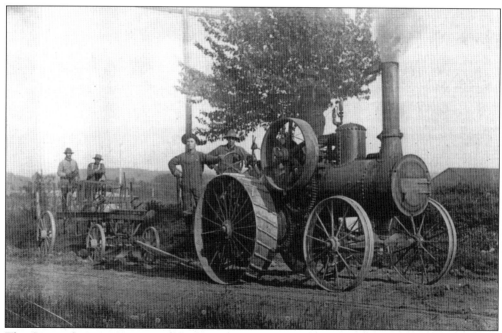

The Swarts farm in Sparta made use of a steam engine that powered a thrashing machine. (Town of Sparta Historian.)

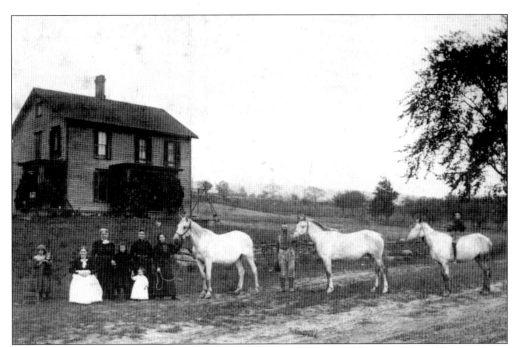

This lovely photograph shows the Hammond family of Sparta with its house and horses about 1895. The little girl at the left has her chair and a doll. There is a chicken in the yard in front of the front porch. (Town of Sparta Historian.)

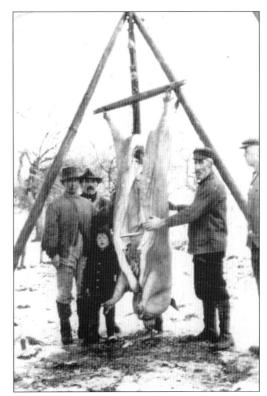

Farms produced much of the meat eaten in nearby towns. This pig from Sparta was probably destined for a Dansville butcher. Dressed, it may have weighed as much as 600 pounds. (Town of Sparta Historian.)

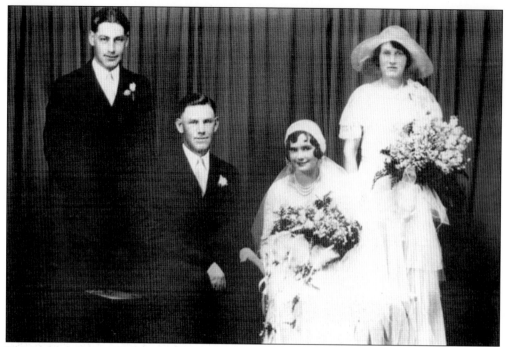

This is the wedding of Henry and Daisy Everman of Sparta in 1938. The folks who plowed and churned and planted and slaughtered also had finery for festive occasions. It is important to note both the hard work and the refined social life on the farms around Dansville. (Town of Sparta Historian.)

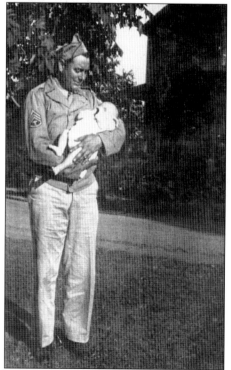

How many times was this scene played out across the United States during World War II? Sergeant Wade of Sparta holds his precious daughter Lucille in 1944. (Town of Sparta Historian.)

This photograph fits the image many Americans have of kids growing up on a farm—two kids in overalls with not a building in sight. They remind the authors of Tom Sawyer and Huckleberry Finn. This was taken in the late 1920s in the town of Ossian. (Russell Kenney.)

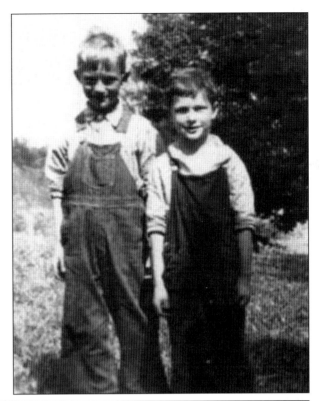

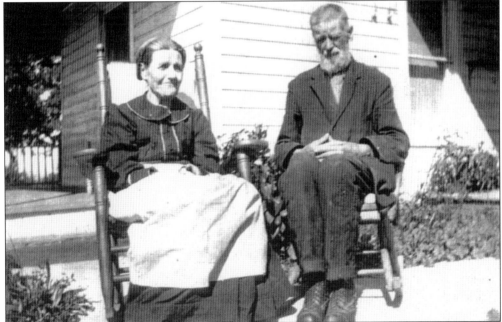

Here are the Meffords of Sparta, rocking in the sun. When people grew old, they did not simply retire and live on Social Security, which was created in 1935, and, of course, they had no pensions. Mrs. Mefford wears an apron, and Mr. Mefford no doubt continued to work on the farm. (Town of Sparta Historian.)

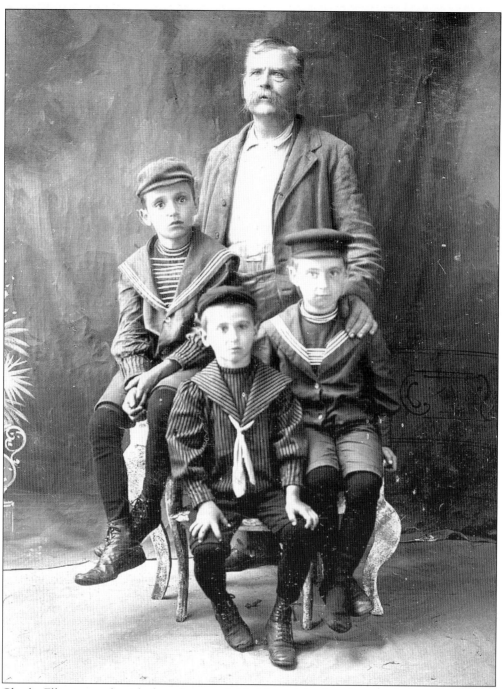

Charlie Ellicott stands with three boys, probably his sons, in this photograph from the town of West Sparta. While he looks like he has just come from a hard day's work, the boys are elegantly attired in these fantastic sailor suits. There must have been something exotic about the sea to those who lived so far from it. (Marion Cosmano.)

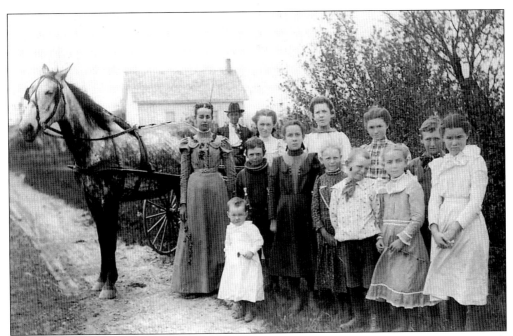

Elementary education in the rural areas took place in one-room schoolhouses, and such schools died out only in the 1950s. For high school, children had to travel to Dansville, as they still do today. Here is the school, school "bus" and driver, faculty, and students of West Sparta's Slaight School District No. 10. (Town of West Sparta Historian.)

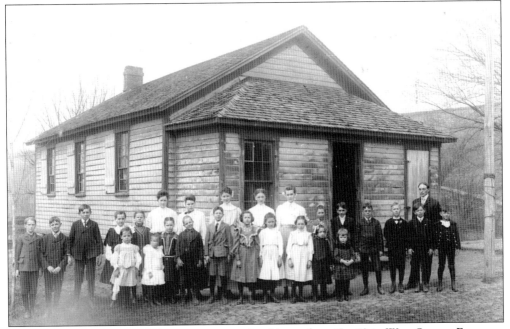

This school in the town of Ossian was somewhat bigger than No. 10 in West Sparta. Everyone wore their Sunday best for this special photograph, although most of these children did chores on their family farms before and after school and normally came to school more humbly dressed. (Town of North Dansville Historian.)

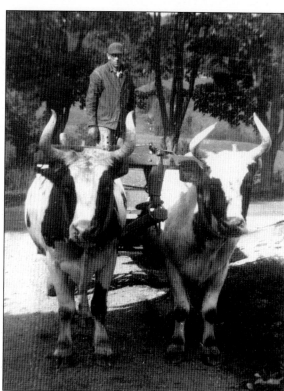

Agricultural products were taken to town by rigs such as this oxcart before trucks replaced them. (Town of North Dansville Historian.)

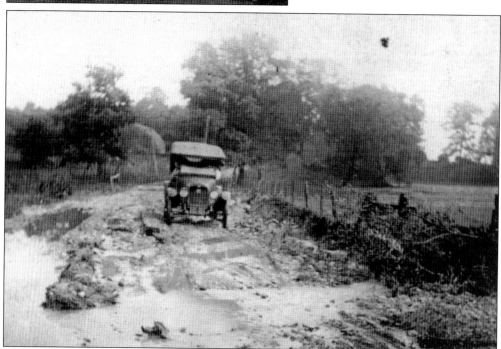

One wonders whether mechanized transport was dependable in the early part of the century. It was not just the engines but the unpaved roads. Here is a car on Logan Hill Road in the town of Sparta in 1918. It speaks more eloquently than any words could. (Town of Sparta Historian.)

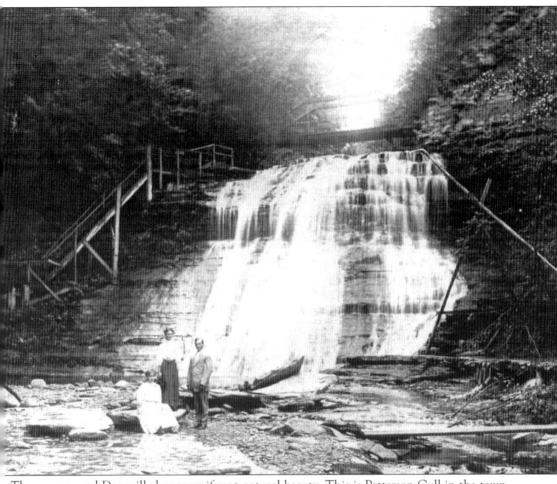

The area around Dansville has magnificent natural beauty. This is Patterson Gull in the town of Sparta. A family is apparently enjoying an outing, which no doubt included a climb to the top and a view from the bridge. (Town of Sparta Historian.)

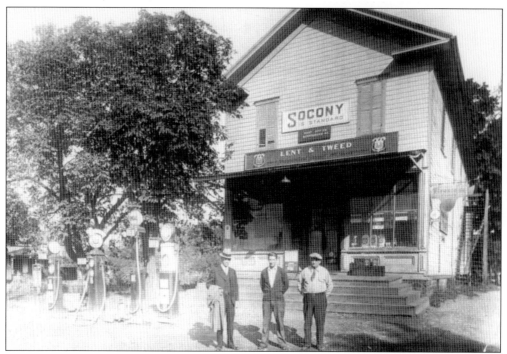

The Lent and Tweed store in the hamlet of Scottsburg in the town of Sparta sold many things. With the coming of the automobile, the proprietors added gasoline and tires (Firestone sign on right side). (Town of Sparta Historian.)

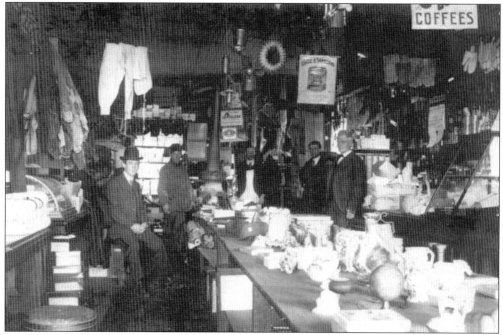

Inside the store is a wide variety of goods from pants to candles. There is a surprisingly large display of decorative porcelain. There is also the potbellied stove where men sat and probably solved most of their and the world's problems. (Town of Sparta Historian.)

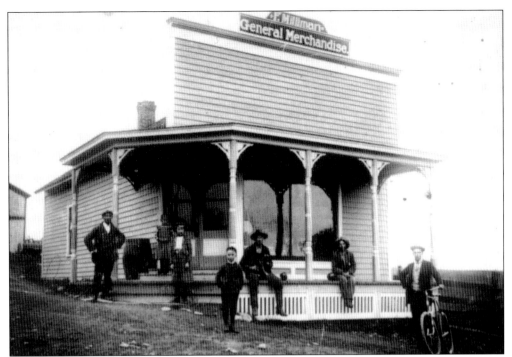

The general stores in rural Livingston County really were general. This is Frank Milliman's store in the hamlet called Bisbeetown in the town of Ossian. (Vince Barron.)

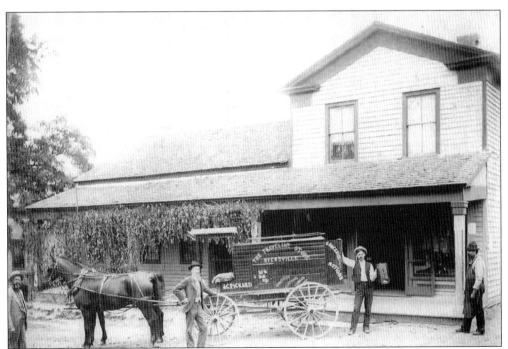

For those who could not conveniently get to a store, a store came to them. This is J. C. Pickard's traveling store operating out of the hamlet of Byersville in the town of West Sparta. (Town of West Sparta Historian.)

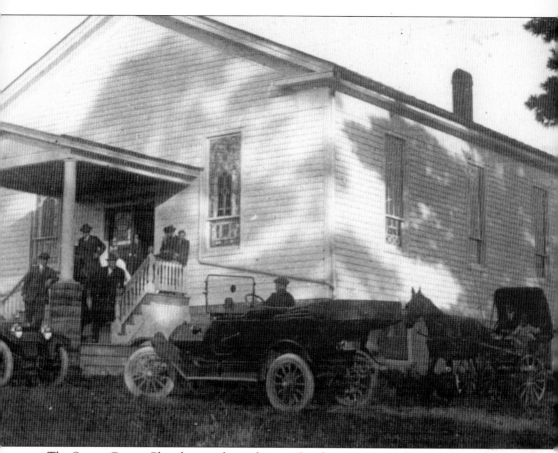

The Sparta Center Church was a busy place on Sunday, as most residents at this time attended the church of their choice. In 1917, some members still came by horse and buggy, but it is clear that the automobile was becoming the common means of local transportation. (Town of North Dansville Historian.)

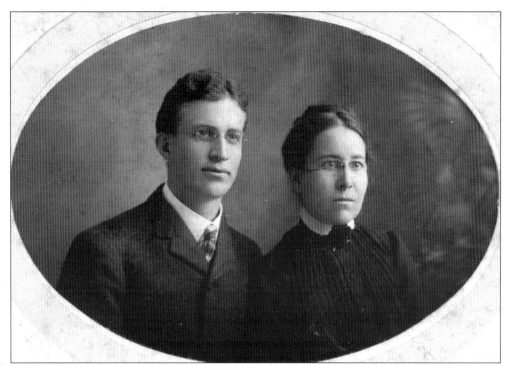

This handsome couple is Rev. John Hubbard and his wife. He was called to the Ossian Presbyterian Church even before his ordination in 1907. Small rural churches often brought very young men to minister to them. In the 21st century, Livingston County's churches are again calling very young ministers, now both males and females, to be their pastors. (Jenny Linzy.)

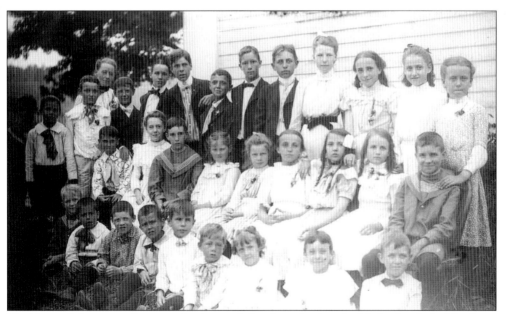

The Epworth League is the name for the youth Sunday school in the Methodist faith. This large group in West Sparta testifies to the importance of religion at the beginning of the 20th century and to the fact that children wore their Sunday best. (Town of West Sparta Historian.)

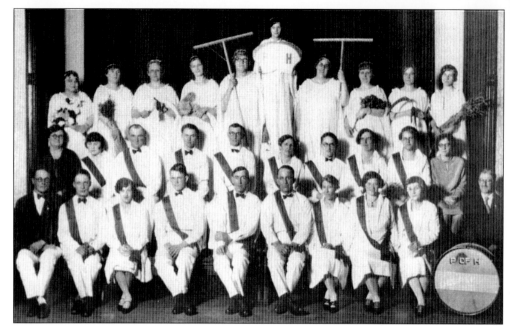

There were social and civic organizations in rural areas, but they had somewhat different characteristics than their counterparts in Dansville. Instead of the Lions or Rotary, there was first and foremost the Grange. This is the degree team of the Scottsburg Grange in the town of Sparta about 1930. The women in the back row hold agricultural implements and products that were used in rituals. The "P of H" on the drum stands for the formal name of the organization, Patrons of Husbandry. (Town of Sparta Historian.)

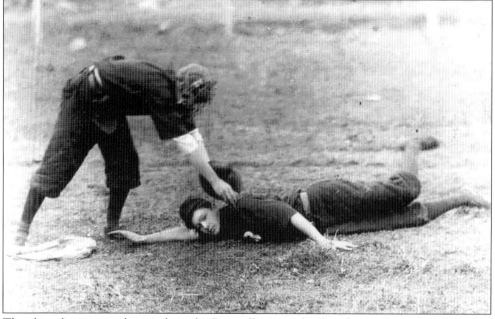

The player being tagged out is from the Byersville team; the B on his uniform is partly visible. Byersville, a hamlet in the town of West Sparta, had a good team, but as this photograph indicates, the baseball diamond was simply a field. (Town of West Sparta Historian.)

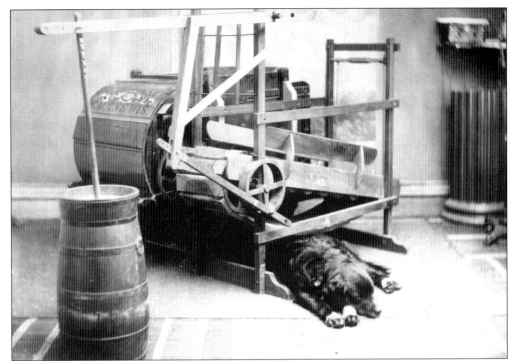

The rural folk were resourceful and were constantly inventing tools and implements to make life easier. There is a wonderful museum today containing many of these tools in the town of West Sparta. This photograph shows a labor-saving device patented by Henry Traxler of Sparta in 1878. It is a dog-powered treadmill that churns butter. Here the dog is resting after some serious churning. (Livingston County Historian.)

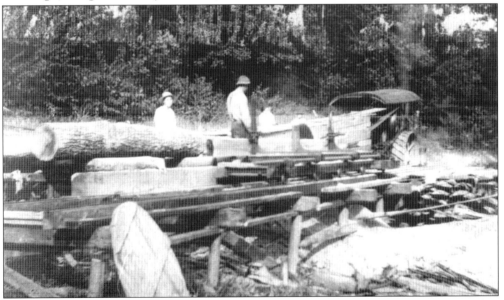

The rural towns produced wood that was used for constructing houses and for many other purposes in Dansville and other towns. This photograph shows the sawmill of Sam Fronk in the town of Sparta. (Town of Sparta Historian.)

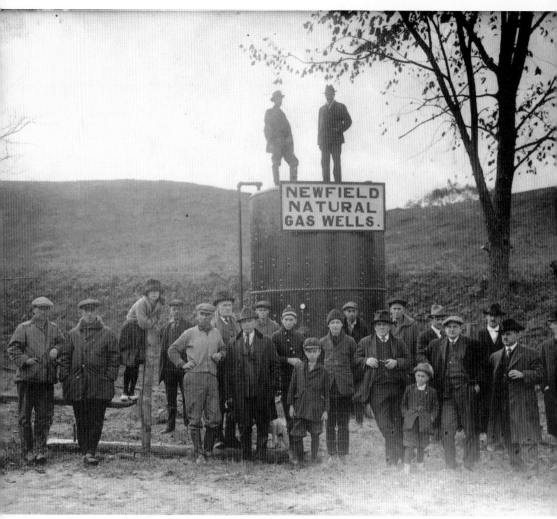

One of the most important stories of the 20th century is the search for fuel. There was hope of finding a large quantity of natural gas near Brodner Creek in the town of West Sparta about 1920. The search did not find a marketable amount. In some way, this symbolizes the history of Dansville and the area around it. There have been numerous attempts to create a prosperous and vibrant community, some of which have failed. Others flourished for a while and then died out. But Dansville is a place of spirit and vibrancy. When something does not pan out, resourceful folks continue to find what will. There may not be gas in West Sparta or a health spa in Dansville, but history tells us that such endings will lead to new attempts and new successes. (Town of North Dansville Historian.)